QUILTING FOR
PEACE

MAKE THE WORLD A BETTER PLACE
ONE STITCH AT A TIME

KATHERINE BELL

PHOTOGRAPHS BY THAYER ALLYSON GOWDY

STC CRAFT | A MELANIE FALICK BOOK
STEWART, TABORI & CHANG
NEW YORK

Table of Contents

CHAPTER ONE

Community Quilting

CHAPTER TWO

Wartime Quilting

Introduction

In the years since September 11, 2001, through faraway wars and natural disasters, economic ups and downs, and my own joys, scares, and disappointments, I developed two quite opposite habits. I obsessively read and watched and worried over the news. And as often as I could, I dropped everything to spend days sewing a quilt as a gift for someone I loved. I wanted to do more to change things and to help those who were suffering, but I didn't know where to start. I found that making quilts helped to alleviate that feeling of being overwhelmed.

Then a couple of things happened that made me realize that my concerns about current events and my love of quilt-making weren't as unrelated as I'd thought. First, my mom sent me a newspaper clipping about a woman in Pennsylvania who'd organized a massive effort to quilt sleeping bags for the homeless. I went to an exhibit at the New England Quilt Museum that included political quilts made by nineteenth-century women, and this exhibit reminded me of the shock of seeing the AIDS Memorial Quilt for the first time in 1995, at the height of the epidemic in the United States. I began to see for myself what generations of quilters have understood: Making quilts is an exceptionally good way to comfort those who need solace, provoke positive change, and provide hope.

Hope—stubborn, human hope—has always been the most effective antidote to fear. And it can be just as contagious. Hope, as Emily Dickinson wrote, keeps so many people warm.

The quilters I know—and especially those I interviewed for this book—are without exception hopeful, resilient people. They're not afraid to acknowledge others' suffering and hardship. And when they spot a problem, no matter how far away or how overwhelming it may seem, they don't allow themselves to be paralyzed. They don't hesitate to try to solve it. More often than not, they work together. They do this with humor and joy. And even if their contributions are small, they have proved again and again that small things, stitched together, add up.

The act of piecing a patchwork quilt is both utterly practical and powerfully symbolic. It's an act of reclaiming, saving, mending, and unifying. The result, the quilt itself, solves a basic problem—the need for warmth—but it represents much more: the quiltmaker's resourcefulness, wishes, and fierce opinions; an attempt to make something beautiful out of what otherwise might have been wasted; and a desire to make some kind of peace.

In the twenty-first century, crafters of all ages are taking to their sewing machines in unprecedented numbers. Spend a little time on crafting websites and blogs, or in one of the hip fabric stores cropping up across the country, and you'll find a network of quilters who are designing and making quilts in inventive ways. Quite a few of them, like the reformist quilters of the nineteenth and early twentieth centuries, use their craft to make political statements, to raise money for the causes that matter to them, and to change people's minds and move them to act.

So this is both a hopeful book and a practical one. You'll find essays about individuals and groups that quilt for peace in many different ways: to help those in need in their communities, to honor veterans, to comfort sick children, to change the world. You'll also find projects for both novice and experienced quilters, some designed to be completed relatively quickly to fulfill an urgent need and some more time-consuming and intricate, meant to show, stitch by stitch, just how much the recipient means to the maker. The imagination and determination of the women and men I interviewed while writing this book inspired me to spend less time worrying and more time making quilts, and to help in whatever small ways I can to make peace. I hope *Quilting for Peace* will do the same for you.

> **"**
>
> 'Hope' is the thing with feathers —
> That perches in the soul —
> And sings the tune without the words —
> And never stops — at all —
>
> And sweetest — in the Gale — is heard —
> And sore must be the storm —
> That could abash the little Bird
> That kept so many warm —
>
> **"**
>
> EMILY DICKINSON
> *From "'Hope' is the thing with feathers"*

CHAPTER ONE

Community Quilting

Quilting bees—sewing parties at which neighbors help each other finish quilts—have been an essential part of North America's past. On the frontier, neighbors had no choice but to depend on each other, but even in the more settled East, nineteenth-century American women developed a firm tradition of cooperatively working to help neighbors who had fallen on sudden hard times, as well as the consistently poor, who didn't then have access to government aid.

In communities large and small across America, women continue to hold quilting bees, though they don't often go by that name anymore. Nearly every quilting guild organizes charity efforts to support its local community, and other groups meet to make quilts for specific recipients: a nearby cancer center, a hospice, or a homeless shelter, for example.

Many contemporary quilters, rather than gathering at each other's houses or at church, meet on the Internet. The members of online quilting groups may be scattered about the country, or even around the globe, but they have a great deal in common with the neighborly quilting bees of the nineteenth century. Women collaborate on quilts by swapping blocks with each other through the mail, and they egg each other on to finish as many quilts as possible. They share sewing tips, jokes, and tales about their families. They ask each other to support causes they care strongly about. And when one among them encounters difficulty herself—a flood, perhaps, or a loved one's death—the other quilters do their best to help.

The projects in this chapter embody the spirit of the quilting bee. They are meant to bring relief to those who need it, and are fittingly practical, such as an old-fashioned tied "comfort" for a family going through a crisis, or a bedroll meant for those sleeping on the streets.

The Sunshine Circle

The Sunshine Circle has been holding quilting meetings in the farming community a couple of miles to the north of tiny Earlham, Iowa, since 1912. More than half of the group's fifteen current members have lived in Earlham all their lives and belong to the circle's second or third generation. Wanda Knight, whose grandmother, mother, and aunt were all involved in the Sunshine Circle, has attended meetings since she was a child, "crawling underneath the quilting frame." For decades, members took turns hosting the group—which often numbered three dozen—at their farmhouses; now they gather in the basement of the Bear Creek Friends Church, a Quaker meetinghouse established by the town's founders in 1856.

Wanda explains that, from its earliest days, the Sunshine Circle's main purpose has been to employ its members' sewing skills for the benefit of others in their community, hand-quilting quilts to raise money for those in need and piecing "comforts" to donate to those who have suffered house fires or other calamities. Contemporary quilters don't always make a distinction between quilts and comforts. Technically, the top, batting, and backing of comforts (also called comforters) are tied together, while quilts are quilted together in decorative patterns, either by hand or machine. Comforts are far less time-consuming to finish than quilts; that's why Sunshine Circle members always tie the patchwork tops they plan to donate.

"I put comforts together, but I always thought that was cheating," Wanda says. She is proud of her hand-quilting skills. "I like to do the little stitches. I try to get at least eleven stitches per inch."

For the hand-quilted quilts, the group begins by unfolding a bed-size wooden quilting frame that stays folded against the wall in the church basement between monthly meetings. They then agree on a quilting design and stretch the quilt across the frame to hold the layers taut, allowing for neat hand-quilting. The quilters sit around the frame's edges, carefully stitching and talking over local news. There are so few quilters—no more than a dozen regularly attend meetings these days, and only a handful of those know how to hand-quilt—it takes many months to finish a quilt, but the Sunshine Circle has plenty of patient customers willing to pay to have their quilts hand-quilted. A small portion of the money earned from these quilts goes toward the church's expenses, a little is occasionally spent on materials, and the rest is donated to nearby charitable organizations, including a women's crisis center and the Earlham food bank, which keeps its stores of food in the basement of the Bear Creek Church near the quilting frame. "We like to help local folks," says Winifred Standing, who joined the group when she and her husband, whose mother and aunts were Sunshine Circle members, moved to Earlham in 1968.

Those who don't hand-quilt spend part of their time during meetings piecing scraps by hand into four-patch blocks. Someone takes the blocks home, machine-pieces them into a full-size top, and then brings the top to the next meeting to be tied into a comfort. When misfortune hits the community—a fire, for example, or a tornado—the group gives a comfort to the afflicted family. In one instance, they gave comforts to the families of those killed and injured in a car crash on the highway into Earlham. After a house fire in nearby DeSoto in which a small boy died, the Circle gave a comfort to the grieving parents. And when Winifred's own hay barn burned down a few years ago, she and her husband received a comfort; they have slept beneath it ever since. For the last twenty years or so, the members of the Sunshine Circle have also tied baby comforts for tiny patients in Iowa hospitals, especially those affected by HIV/AIDS or substance abuse. Because of the baby comforts' small size, the women can tie three or four in a single meeting.

The monthly meetings have not changed a great deal over the years. On the second Wednesday of every month—except August and December—the quilters meet around 10 A.M. and stay until mid-afternoon. Whoever is the hostess for the month makes the coffee and tea and brings dessert, and the members bring their own sack lunches. "We just have such a good time visiting and working together," Winifred says. "Part of the fun is eating together and seeing what we have as a treat." After lunch, the secretary reads the minutes from the previous meeting, the members go over any other business, and then they set to work again.

The circle's membership has dwindled over the years, from a peak of thirty-five in the late 1960s and early 1970s to about a dozen, and most of the current members are in their seventies or eighties. "It's hard to draw in young women," Winifred explains. The fact that meetings are held on weekdays prevents women with nine-to-five jobs from attending. Plus, hand-quilting and hand-piecing are vanishing skills; the younger generation prefers machine-quilting. But for those who still attend, the Sunshine Circle is a way to maintain the sort of deep local connections and neighborly support that have always anchored their farming community. "It's a wonderful time to get together with neighbors," Wanda says. Winifred agrees: "When we get together and visit, when we talk about people that aren't there, it isn't gossip. People are caring about how other people are getting along, what's happening in their families. It's just a very warm hearted group." And as it has for almost a century, the quilters' caring extends far beyond the perimeter of their small circle. ✳

SUNSHINE CIRCLE MINUTES

Throughout its history, the Sunshine Circle has kept minutes of its meetings.

On March 11, 1914: "The afternoon was spent in tying comforts for Mr. and Mrs. Weekley on account of their home being burned. The material being donated except the cotton for one comfort, which came to 56 cents to be paid by members of the circle who did not donate Material...It was decided for the Pres. and Sec. to deliver the comforts and also fruit which was donated. 22 qts. in all."

Twenty years later: "The Sunshine Circle met March 14 (1934) at the home of Stella Williamson. About 25 members were present. The placing committee report some bedding and little boys clothes were placed with Lambs, near Dexter, their house burned recently."

And another fifty-four years later: "Sunshine Circle met April 13, 1988 at the meeting house. A total of 13 members worked on quilts and baby comforters. 10 enjoyed the noon meal and lemon dessert provided by Hazel Steward and Marie Cook...A get well note was written to Erma Inman who was ill with flu. A thank you note from Bertha Osborn was read."

From *Patchwork: Iowa Quilts and Quilters* by Jacqueline Andre Schmeal, University of Iowa Press, 2003.

Four-Patch Comfort

ADAPTED FROM A PATTERN CREATED BY THE SUNSHINE CIRCLE

This tied patchwork comfort is a good project for a group of quilters to work on together. Sunshine Circle members hand-piece the four-patch blocks and then stitch them together by machine, but I machine-stitched the entire quilt top. Shirting prints (tiny black, blue, or brown prints against a white background) give the comfort an old-fashioned feel.

FINISHED SIZE

78 inches x 91 inches

WHAT YOU'LL NEED

2½ yards of 44-inch-wide quilting cotton in each of two solid colors (for quilt top)

1¼ yards of 44-inch-wide quilting cotton in four shirting prints (for quilt top)

7½ yards of 44-inch-wide quilting cotton (for backing)

Full-size (93 inches x 96 inches) cotton batting

2 skeins pearl cotton

Curved hand-sewing needle

SEWING INSTRUCTIONS

1. Cut seventeen 4-inch-deep, selvedge-to-selvedge strips from each of the two solid fabrics and nine 4-inch-deep, selvedge-to-selvedge strips from each of the prints. Cut each strip into ten 4-inch squares. Set two squares of each solid and six squares of each print aside (28 squares total)—they're extras.

2. Choose one solid square and one print square. With right sides together and their edges aligned, sew the pair together along one edge with a ¼-inch seam. Repeat 41 times, without cutting the thread between each pair of squares (this process is called chain-piecing). After sewing the 42 pairs, snip the threads close to the first and last stitch of each seam, and press the seam allowances on each pair together toward the darker fabric.

3. Repeat step 2 with the same solid fabric and each of the three remaining prints.

4. Repeat steps 2 and 3 with the second solid fabric.

5. With right sides together and the edges aligned, sew two matching pairs of squares together, with the print squares placed diagonally opposite each other, being careful to line up the center seams. Then press the seam allowances together to one side (it doesn't matter which direction you press the seams at this stage since there will be lighter and darker fabrics on both sides). Using your square transparent ruler, trim the block to 7 inches square. Be sure to keep the intersection of four patches at the center of each block.

6. Repeat step 5 until you have 168 four-patch blocks.

7. Lay the blocks out in 14 rows of 12 blocks, alternating the solid blocks so that you form diagonal lines of each color.

8. With right sides together and their edges aligned, sew the blocks into rows, using a ¼-inch seam and carefully matching the center seam of each block. Press the seam allowances to one side.

9. With right sides together and their edges aligned, sew the rows together with a ¼-inch seam to complete the quilt top. As you sew, match every seam, pinching the two layers of fabric together at each intersection to keep the seams aligned until they reach your sewing machine's presser foot. Press the seam allowances together to either side.

10. Layer the quilt top, batting, and backing to make a quilt sandwich; and pin-baste the sandwich to hold it in place (see page 128).

11. Using a curved hand-sewing needle and pearl cotton, and starting at the center of the quilt and working outward, tie the comforter at the center and all four corners of each four-patch block. To make each tie, insert your needle from the quilt top through the backing, being sure to pierce all three layers. Then bring the needle back up to the quilt top about ⅛ inch away, and cut the pearl cotton leaving a 2-inch tail on each thread. Tie the tails in a square knot (see page 132), and then trim them to ½ inch.

12. Bind the comfort with a mock binding, following the instructions on page 130.

Beloved Quilts

The first quilt Pascha Griffiths made was for a boy she had a crush on in high school. "I needed to express how I felt," she says, "so I made a quilt." Now a thirty-five-year-old mother of two, with seventeen years of quilt-making behind her, Pascha still thinks of her quilts as physical manifestations of love. She's founded a project called Beloved Quilts, through which she gathers volunteers to make and distribute quilts to people made homeless by poverty or violence. The word *beloved* is emblazoned across each quilt.

The idea came to her in 2005, when she was pregnant with her second child. She was cleaning the house, snacking on tortilla chips, and stressing out about what her pregnancy would mean for the Possibilities Factory, a nonprofit organization that held after-school programs and leadership camps for kids—she'd started it in 2000 and put it on hold after her first baby. As a member of the Vineyard, an evangelical church she describes as "contemporary, apolitical, and really into social justice," Pascha had a down-to-earth relationship with God. Still, when she asked out loud what she should do next with her life, she was surprised by the answer: "Stop eating tortilla chips," she heard.

"It's not what you expect God to say," she says, laughing, adding that the instruction seemed so definite she spit out the chips. When she unwrapped a new roll of paper towels

to clean up the mess, she noticed the words "big quilts" printed on the wrapper. "Right away I knew," she says, "I was going to make quilts for the homeless." Pascha had been concerned about homelessness ever since college, when a brief bout of frostbite after an afternoon of sledding heightened her awareness of one of the dangers of living without shelter. She later volunteered for agencies serving the homeless and, never quite shaking the memory of her own frozen toes, held parties to collect donations of socks.

A foil emergency blanket can keep a person warm, but Pascha wanted her quilts to accomplish much more than that. "You wouldn't skimp on a quilt you were making for your parent or your child," Pascha says. She wanted to wrap each recipient in a message of respect and love, and she wanted that message to be contagious to anyone who worked on or saw one of her quilts. Pascha and her husband Paul came up with a design together: a forty-inch central square with the word *beloved* appliquéd across it, surrounded by patchwork and backed by fleece. She set a goal to organize volunteers to make 100 twin and crib quilts for shelters in the greater Boston area.

Pascha describes the next few months as "an experience of abundance." She wrote to fleece manufacturers asking for donations; one, Malden Mills, donated enough heavy-duty fleece to back all 100 quilts. It took Pascha two trips in her minivan to get it all home. In early 2006, she began recruiting volunteers through her church and her network of friends, and she set up a blog to chronicle and publicize the project. She received a grant from the Massachusetts Art Council, and several people donated sewing machines. A busy local ice cream shop offered to display the quilts to help raise awareness, and Pascha even convinced the security officers at the Massachusetts State House to let her run her finished quilts through their metal detectors to check for errant pins.

People were just as generous with their time. Pascha organized regular sew-ins at her church, where an assembly line of volunteers turned center squares into finished quilts. Not everyone knew how to quilt; Pascha welcomed anyone who could wield a pair of scissors and taught interested beginners how to work a sewing machine. One sew-in led to another. Friends and friends of friends threw quilting parties. A 4-H club made a project of creating center squares. An eighth-grade class made a batch of quilts from start to finish, and a kindergarten class decorated center squares with glitter paint. As Pascha had hoped, quilters added their own touches to the basic design. A retired sea captain spelled *beloved* in patchwork semaphore flags. One quilter appliquéd the word in Spanish, another in graffiti lettering. By the summer of 2007, volunteers had completed forty quilts.

That August, a secret shelter for battered women in Boston was forced to close after a two-alarm fire gutted its top floor. The residents, seventeen women and children who had already been traumatized and made homeless by domestic violence, lost the few things they owned as well as their temporary home. Within days, Pascha delivered seventeen Beloved quilts—the first to be given away—to the shelter's displaced residents. Her husband, Paul, wrote on their shared blog, "Home is more than a building. We want to provide a traveling piece of home these recipients can take with them during a transient time in their lives. A simple, but dignifying action."

Since that summer, Pascha and her volunteers have made many more quilts and given them to a local homeless action coalition to distribute, as well as to nearby women's shelters. On three occasions, Pascha has given quilts personally to homeless people panhandling at the side of the road.

In May 2008, she wrote on her blog:

> In other news, I had the amazing pleasure of giving one of our quilts to a man in the rain. It was such a profound experience for me. This man was standing on the yellow dividing line on Memorial Drive in Cambridge, asking for money. I was driving and thinking, "Darn, I don't think I have anything to give him," and then, "WAIT, I HAVE QUILTS IN MY TRUNK!!!" So, I pulled over into a gas station, and opened up our banged-up back-end of our mini-van, and gave him a quilt. IT WAS AWESOME! He told me that he just got himself into a house and that he was so excited to have this quilt because his other one is totally tattered and falling apart.

In February 2009, Beloved Quilts reachd Pascha's original goal of making 100 quilts for local homeless people. Now the organization has started making quilts for girls who have escaped from child sex trafficking. In 2006, the United Nations Children's Fund estimated that 1.2 million children worldwide are sold for sex or labor every year—that's two children sold into slavery every minute. Pascha decided to do something to help after learning about Love146, a nonprofit based in New Haven, Connecticut, that works to prevent the trafficking of children, and builds and staffs "safehomes" that care for children who have been sexually exploited in Thailand, the Philippines, Cambodia, and India. "How unloved these girls must feeland how tainted their concept of love must be," says Pascha, who wonders what "bed" must mean to them after what has happened to them there. "Then to think that there's this blanket that says they are beloved. They might be too wounded for it to mean anything, but it might mean something. It's one way of saying, 'You're seen, and here's some safety.'" ✳

> **"**
>
> America is not like a blanket—one piece of unbroken cloth, the same color, the same texture, the same size. America is more like a quilt—many patches, many pieces, many colors, many sizes, all woven and held together by a common thread.
>
> **"**
>
> JESSE JACKSON

The Sleeping Bag Project

On any given night in America, an estimated three quarters of a million people are homeless. Just over half stay in shelters or transitional housing. The rest sleep in cars, in doorways, under bridges, in cardboard boxes—wherever they can find a relatively sheltered spot. Most will manage to secure a place to live within a few months, only to be replaced on the streets and in the shelters by others who have fallen on difficult times.

Homeless people outnumber shelter beds in every major U.S. city, which means that each night many are turned away at shelter doors. The luckiest of these are given a potentially lifesaving gift: a handmade sleeping bag. Across America, a loose network of volunteers makes portable bedrolls out of recycled fabric and blankets and donates them to agencies that serve the homeless, and occasionally directly to homeless people themselves. The Sleeping Bag Project is the life's work of Flo Wheatley, a former nurse in rural Pennsylvania. Flo, her husband, Jim, their three children, and an ever-expanding army of volunteers have been making and distributing sleeping bags—or ugly quilts, as they affectionately call them—since 1980.

In those years, the Sleeping Bag Project has grown from a family endeavor to an international grassroots effort. It's impossible to count the number of volunteers involved in the project, because the Wheatleys have kept it informal and decentralized. That's intentional; they don't want paperwork or anything else to slow down the production of sleeping bags. For years, the pattern has been copied and passed from quilter to quilter; and it has been posted on the Internet since its inception. Flo knows that at least 100,000 sleeping bags are donated every year, but the number, she says, may be much higher.

Flo became acutely aware of the problem of homelessness in the late 1970s, when, at age fourteen, her son Leonard was diagnosed with non-Hodgkin's lymphoma. After doctors at a local hospital gave him six weeks to live, Leonard began an intensive schedule of chemotherapy at Sloan Kettering Cancer Center in Manhattan. Flo and her son stayed with her niece in Queens during the week and went home to their Pennsylvania farm on the weekends. One Monday, as Flo was trying to maneuver Leonard and their luggage out of a cab and into the subway in the pouring rain, the boy collapsed. As she propped her son up, Flo heard a voice say, "Lady, you need help." "No, I'm fine," she said, "I just need to get to the subway." A few minutes later, the same voice said again, "Lady, you need help." It belonged to a tall, thin man wearing an army jacket and gold-rimmed glasses without any lenses. Before Flo could protest, he hoisted her suitcase onto his shoulder and took off down the stairs into the subway. She rallied Leonard and followed. The man rode two trains with Flo and Leonard and then hailed them a cab. Just before they drove away, he leaned into the window and said softly, "Don't abandon me," words, Flo says, that "went right to my toes. I still had a job to do—I still had to get my son to my niece's house—so we carried on. But I couldn't get over what he said. I have chills even now just thinking about it."

A year and a half later, Leonard's health was beginning to improve. On one of their less frequent trips into the city, as they crossed the 59th Street Bridge, Flo saw a man lying against an abutment, wrapped in a bright pink crocheted blanket. She imagined that someone had made that blanket expressly for him. As soon as she returned home, Flo asked her kids to bring her any clothes they no longer needed. ("We're not rich people," she says. "We had to use what we had.") She cut and pieced fabric from the clothing into two big squares, layered old blankets in between, and sewed around the edges. She folded this rough quilt in half, stitched it together to form a sleeping bag, rolled it up, and tied it with a couple of her husband's cast-off ties. Jim then drove into Manhattan and gave it away to the first homeless man he saw. The Wheatleys gave eight sleeping bags away the first year, and more the second. They were made entirely out of recycled fabric, just like the first one, with more regard for warmth, portability, and durability than beauty.

"We didn't realize anyone knew what we were doing," Flo says. But by the end of the second year, neighbors began dropping by to offer fabric, and then a local church invited Flo and Jim to demonstrate their sleeping-bag-making process to a gathering of potential volunteers. After that, Flo held workshops at churches, schools, and Scout groups. As Flo explained in a 1995 article in *Family Circle* magazine, she named the bags "ugly quilts" in order "to make sure that volunteers weren't scared off by the quilting part. We wanted people to say, 'That's how I can help!' just as I did when I saw that homeless man wrapped in the pink blanket." The Wheatleys bought a van, and Jim began driving the three hours from the farm into New York twice a week to deliver sleeping bags to shelters and homeless camps.

In 1994, more than a decade after the project began, the popular spiritual magazine *Guideposts* published an article about the Sleeping Bag Project, and the project grew exponentially. Thousands of letters, requests for information, donated material, and finished sleeping bags arrived at the Wheatleys' farm every week. They converted the barn into a warehouse, and Flo began making breakfast once a week for the "Wednesday Crew"—a group of volunteers, mostly women, who came to open mail and sort donations. The Sleeping Bag Project began distributing not only sleeping bags but donated clothes, hats and mittens, underwear, and socks to those living on the streets in cities in neighboring states. "We are totally hypothermia-oriented," Flo says.

After she and Jim retired, they turned all of their time and attention to the organization, and Leonard, who survived his childhood cancer, has always helped out as well. These days, Jim and Flo personally distribute about 6,000 sleeping bags a year, sometimes delivering fifty or a hundred at once to a shelter. Flo guesses that most ugly quilts don't last more than a winter, although she knows of one exceptional group of homeless people who live under a bridge in Manhattan, who asked a church to put on a bake sale for them so they could rent a room in which to store their sleeping bags over the summer.

After well over two decades, the project began to outlive some of the original volunteers. "As the years went on," Flo says, "we were a little worried about how this would carry on. But as the older generation is leaving us, the young people are picking up the slack, and that's been our saving grace." All over the country, high school and college groups, summer camps, and Scout troops have taken up the cause. And a brand-new website, www.thesleepingbagproject.org, is getting the word out to an even bigger audience.

Throughout the years, Flo and Jim have stuck firmly to two principles: First, the sleeping bags have to be utterly simple, with easy measurements and a minimum of sewing. "It's still a kitchen-table project," Flo says. "It has to be, so that people aren't afraid to try it." One person can make a simple ugly quilt in a day; a group can do it in an hour. She wants to keep it that way, she says, so that anyone from fifth grade up can participate, regardless of previous sewing experience.

Second, it's possible to make and donate these sleeping bags without spending any money. They're made entirely out of recycled materials—whatever volunteers have on hand. As Flo travels around the Eastern seaboard, giving workshops and visiting shelters, she carries donated supplies with her to share with volunteers wherever she can. The donated embroidery needles that she gives to volunteers for tying the quilts are often dull, but they work. And hotels often donate bed linens, which they're required by law to replace on a regular basis. Sleeping Bag Project volunteers are urged to give the bags they make to shelters in their hometowns, which saves on distribution costs. There are homeless people everywhere, Flo says, so volunteers should serve those "in their own backyard."

Occasionally, however, volunteers have good reasons to ignore that recommendation. During the Kosovo refugee crisis in the late 1990s, for example, U.S. Air Force officers' wives based in Germany made sleeping bags and put them on the planes that dropped supplies for the refugees. And a group of English widows, remembering their own experiences during World War II, made sleeping bags and drove them all the way to the Balkans.

When Flo talks about the runaway success and extraordinary reach of her idea, she sounds modest and pleased, but not entirely surprised. Ever practical, she reminds volunteers again and again of the group's basic goal, which has not changed in nearly three decades: to keep the homeless warm until they can be helped or healed by others. Flo's singleness of purpose and her matter-of-fact view of the world have allowed the Sleeping Bag Project to grow exponentially without ever losing what made it successful in the first place: its utter simplicity. ✳

HOW YOU CAN HELP

Make a sleeping bag out of recycled fabrics using the instructions on the facing page, and donate it to a nearby homeless shelter. If possible, include a man's winter coat, hat, or mittens in the sleeping bag before rolling it up, as warm clothing is always needed.

Find nearby homeless shelters by calling your local United Way office. Visit their website at www.liveunited.org to find a location near you.

To donate fabric to the Sleeping Bag Project or to identify other ways that you can volunteer, visit www.thesleepingbagproject.org.

Recycled Sleeping Bag

ADAPTED FROM THE SLEEPING BAG PROJECT PATTERN

This pattern was designed with input from people who have slept on the streets. It's big enough to fit a fully clothed adult, or even a parent and child, and is warm but not so heavy it's difficult to carry. Use recycled fabric or take the opportunity to make a dent in your stash, choosing dark colors that won't show dirt. The sleeping bag pictured on pages 20 and 21 includes a couple of old sheets and worn wool blankets, as well as fabric left over from another quilting project.

FINISHED SIZE
3½ feet x 7 feet

WHAT YOU'LL NEED

Large pieces of recycled cotton or poly/cotton fabric (clean sheets and duvet covers work well) in medium or dark colors

A couple of clean, used blankets—one wool blanket plus one fleece blanket or mattress pad is ideal (resist the urge to keep adding blankets since too much wool makes the bag too heavy)

Matching cotton thread

Crochet cotton

Tapestry needle with large eye

4 yards of ⅞-inch-wide grosgrain ribbon in any color, or recycle two men's ties

SEWING INSTRUCTIONS

1. Align and machine-sew together enough pieces of fabric to form a piece slightly larger than 7 feet square; then trim the fabric to a 7-foot square. Repeat the process to make a second 7-foot square.

2. With right sides together, sew the squares at one end with a ½-inch seam, forming approximately a 7-foot x 14-foot rectangle.

3. Cut the ribbon in half and fold each piece in half. On one short side of the fabric rectangle, make two chalk marks, one 7 inches from the left edge and another 14 inches from the same edge.

4. Pin the folded edge of each piece of ribbon to the wrong side of the fabric at the two marked spots (see Diagram A on page 21). Machine-stitch a box with an X inside it to secure each ribbon (see Diagram B on page 21).

5. Lay the sleeping-bag rectangle right side down on the floor, smooth it out, and use a few pieces of masking tape along each side to hold it in place.

6. Trim the blankets/mattress pad to measure 6½ feet wide x 6 feet 9 inches high. Layer them on half of the sleeping-bag rectangle, with one 6½-foot edge against the center seam, leaving a 3-inch seam allowance on each of the three open sides (see Diagram C on page 21).

(A)

Fabric's
wrong side

(B)

Ribbon tie

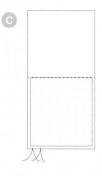

(C)

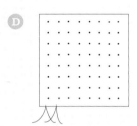

(D)

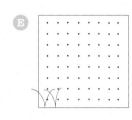

(E)

(F)

(G)

Fold the half of the rectangle that's a single layer of fabric over the half that's covered with the blankets/mattress pad, and smooth the fabric in place.

7. Thread the tapestry needle with a doubled length of crochet cotton. Then stitch into and out of the sleeping bag every 10 inches, using square knots (see page 132) at each stitching point to tie and secure the lining (see Diagram D). Cut ½-inch tails on each tie.

8. Fold the ribbons up onto the tied fabric (see Diagram E).

9. Fold the tied fabric in half lengthwise, forming a 7-foot x 3½-foot sleeping bag. The top opening and one side seam will be automatically finished.

10. To close the bag's remaining side and bottom edges, tie and triple-knot the doubled crochet cotton every 3 inches along these edges,

positioning the knots close to the filling and being sure to catch all four layers of fabric (see Diagram F). Leave the edges raw.

11. Turn the sleeping bag right side out. Fold it in half lengthwise. Starting from the open top end, roll the sleeping bag up, and tie the ribbon ties tightly (see Diagram G).

HeartStrings Quilt Project

More than a century after quilters discovered sewing machines, they have fallen in love with another technology: the Internet. Today, tens of thousands of quilters exchange patterns, blog about their projects, swap blocks, join online quilting guilds, and recruit each other to quilt for people in need. On Yahoo alone, there are more than 4,000 quilting groups, and several hundred of these are involved in charity quilting. The mission of one of the most popular Yahoo groups, Stashbuster, is to help fellow quilters come up with ways to quilt through their backlogs of fabric.

In 2006, a group of Stashbuster members decided to make quilts to donate to a variety of charities. They made string quilts—in which each block is made of strips of leftover fabric sewn to a fabric foundation—because they're easy and fun, and they're a good way to use up small scraps of fabric. Twenty or so quilters enjoyed the charity project so much they formed their own online group, HeartStrings, devoted entirely to making string quilts for people in need.

Rather than making quilts for a specific cause, HeartStrings volunteers decide exactly where to donate the quilts they make. "That's something that makes us successful," coordinator Mary Johnson says, "because everyone has certain charities they feel a connection to." Members donate to hospitals, shelters, and nursing homes in their own hometowns, as well as to national organizations like the Ronald McDonald House, which supports the families of chronically ill children; Project Linus, a nationwide effort to provide hand-knitted and sewn blankets to kids in need; and Quilts of Valor (see page 44), an organization that makes quilts for soldiers returning from Iraq and Afghanistan.

In its first eighteen months, 600 quilters from all over the world joined HeartStrings. Today, Mary Johnson and Sue Frank, both of Minneapolis, Minnesota, coordinate the group's activities in the United States. Sue collects blocks from volunteers and, with the help of her mother, sews them into quilt tops. Mary machine-quilts and finishes tops, donates those she finishes, and manages the HeartStrings blog and message boards. In Kelmscott, in Western Australia, Stephanie Driel collects blocks donated by Australian quilters and turns them into finished quilts. Members quilt at their own paces, and many of them choose to finish quilts by themselves and give them away locally. Some mail the coordinators a block or two on occasion, others request blocks from the coordinators and assemble tops out of them, and a handful of accomplished machine quilters concentrate on quilting tops others have pieced. The last quilter to work on a collaboratively made quilt decides where to donate it. When quilters piece individual blocks, they always put a red or a blue stripe in the center. Because of that, blocks made by different quilters out of different styles of fabric can coexist perfectly well in a single quilt.

Often, members recruit each other to make quilts for causes important to them. When one member's son returned from the war in Iraq, she rallied HeartStrings members to make quilts for twenty-eight soldiers in his company who didn't have family waiting for them. At times, the whole group embarks on a monthlong project. Sometimes these projects coincide with other organizations' efforts to raise awareness about a particular issue. In October 2007, for example, the group marked National Breast Cancer Awareness Month by making pink string quilts for women fighting breast cancer. Other monthlong challenges are simply meant to encourage members to make a greater number of quilts by focusing on a particular group of recipients (like kids in need) or a new pattern (like the Chinese Coin pattern, made from long strips pieced from short fabric strings, rather than the square blocks used in standard HeartStrings quilts). Members foster a healthy sense of competition by posting updates on their progress and photographs of their completed quilts on the HeartStrings website.

Many HeartStrings quilts are given to individuals rather than organizations. When a member of the group hears of a neighbor's misfortune or illness, for example, she will make sure that person receives a quilt. Mary gives an example of a HeartStrings member who posted a note on the group's message board about a family she knew who had lost everything in a house fire. After Mary sent quilts to the family's two little girls, she received an e-mail from the quilter who had posted the message; she described the parents' tears upon receiving the quilts that morning at church. "It's a very personal connection," Mary says.

Personal connections are what HeartStrings is all about. And thanks to the Internet, they're made across great distances between people who have never met—between the givers and recipients of quilts, and also among the quilters. On the group's online discussion forum, members share quilting techniques and inspiration and participate in "virtual sew days," during which they continually check in online to compare notes about the quilts they're working on. Perhaps most importantly, they share details of their lives with each other. "You get to know what's going on in their lives, if they're having health problems or family issues," Mary says. "It's a community, so there's a lot of support." ✳

HOW YOU CAN HELP

HeartStrings suggests making a string quilt to donate to a charity of your choice (see the string quilt pattern on page 24). Alternatively, donate individual blocks to a HeartStrings coordinator who will arrange to have them sewn into a quilt with other donated blocks.

Join the HeartStrings Yahoo group, **www.groups.yahoo.com/group/ HeartStringsQuiltProject**, to volunteer to piece a top or finish a quilt.

Visit **www.heartstringsquiltproject.com** for more information and to find other ways you can contribute.

Pink Ribbon String Quilt

ADAPTED FROM A HEARTSTRINGS QUILT PROJECT PATTERN

HeartStrings Quilt Project recommends that you make a string quilt and donate it to the charity of your choice. I chose to make a quilt for a breast cancer patient. This quilt is big enough to curl up under but small enough to carry to chemotherapy sessions. The pink stripes at the center of the blocks in this quilt pay homage to the pink ribbons worn to raise awareness for breast cancer.

FINISHED SIZE

54 inches x 72 inches

WHAT YOU'LL NEED

For quilt top

3½ yards of 44-inch-wide muslin (for foundation)

1½ yards of pale pink, 44-inch-wide quilting cotton

½ yard each of six 44-inch-wide, printed pink and grey quilting cottons

¾ yard of printed pink 44-inch-wide quilting cotton

¾ yard of solid grey 44-inch-wide quilting cotton

Matching cotton thread

For backing

5 yards of 44-inch-wide quilting cotton
(pale solid shade works well)

For binding

½ yard of 44-inch-wide quilting cotton

Twin size (93-inch x 72-inch) cotton batting

12½-inch-square transparent quilter's ruler

SEWING INSTRUCTIONS

1. From the muslin, cut forty-eight 10-inch squares. You'll build the blocks on these foundation squares.

2. Cut the solid pink fabric into 2-inch-deep selvedge-to-selvedge strips.

3. Cut the remaining pink and grey fabrics into selvedge-to-selvedge strips ranging from 1½ inches to 3 inches deep.

4. Place a solid pink strip, right side up, diagonally across the center of a square of muslin, and trim the ends of the strip so that they extend just past the foundation square's corners. Next place one of any of the grey or pink printed fabric strips, right side down, on the solid pink strip, lining up one long edge of the second strip with one long edge of the solid pink strip (see Diagram A on page 27). Again trim the ends of the second strip, so they extend just past the edges of the muslin foundation. Sew along the aligned edges of the two strips with a ¼-inch seam. Unfold the top strip, so it's right side up, and press it flat.

5. Place another of the printed grey or pink strips, right side down, on the other side of the center strip, aligning one of its long edges with the center strip's long edge and trimming its ends just beyond the foundation square's corners. As in step 4, sew the new strip in place with a ¼-inch seam, unfold the strip so that it's right side up, and press it flat (see Diagram B).

6. Continue to add printed grey or pink strips on either side of the center strip, aligning, trimming, and sewing them as before until you have covered the entire foundation.

7. Press the block, and then trim it to 9½ inches square so that the center strip runs evenly through the two corners it covers. To trim the block accurately, use a square transparent quilter's ruler, and make sure that the 1-inch squares running along the ruler's central diagonal line fit perfectly along the center strip's full length (see Diagram C). (Note that if your ruler is configured with right-angle lines, not squares, make sure the center diagonal line runs straight down the center of the center strip.)

8. Repeat steps 4 through 7, continually varying the order in which you place the grey and pink fabrics around the solid-pink center strip, until you have 48 blocks.

9. Arrange the blocks in eight rows of six blocks. Using a ¼-inch seam, sew the blocks together into rows, and then sew the rows together.

10. Make a quilt sandwich (see page 128). Then, beginning in the center and moving outward to prevent rippling, machine-quilt the sandwich with a grid or an allover meandering pattern (see page 130).

11. Bind the quilt with a traditional binding (see pages 129–130).

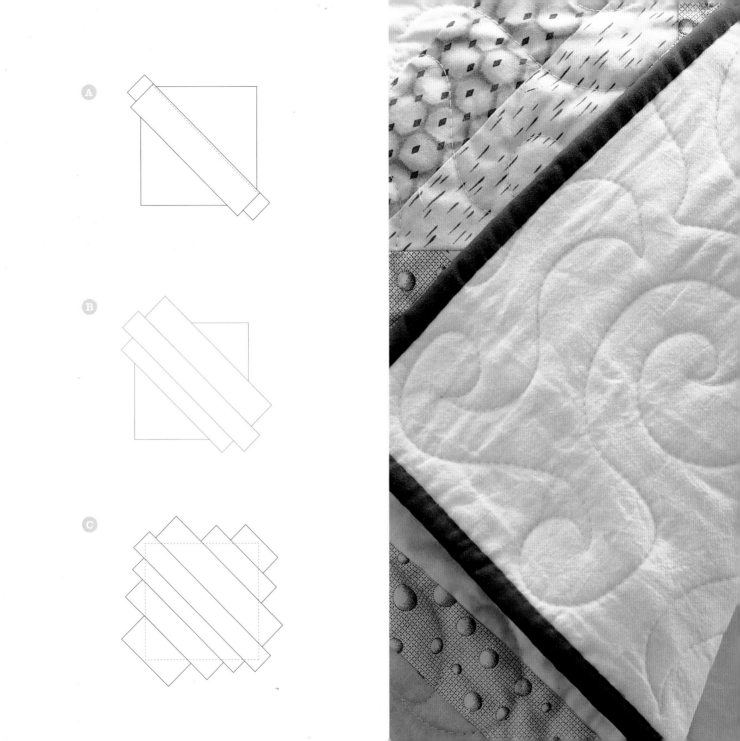

Mother's Comfort Project

In New York City, three shelters run by Animal Care and Control take in 44,000 animals, mostly dogs and cats, each year. The shelters, along with local animal advocacy groups, work hard to improve the prospects for New York's homeless animals. In recent years, they've more than doubled the number of animals adopted and halved the euthanasia rate. One factor in that success is their cage comforter program, which encourages volunteers to sew simple, comfy beds to comfort dogs and cats and brighten their cages.

Krysta Vollbrecht works at one animal welfare organization, the Farm Sanctuary, and volunteers at another, Rational Animal. When Rational Animal's founder, Susan Brandt, decided to rally volunteers to make cage comforters for the city's shelters, Krysta offered to organize the project. She didn't have any sewing experience, but she knew she could find people who did. "I have a lot of friends who are crafty people," she says. "I knew I could help find materials and get people who know how to sew together."

The Mother's Comfort Project, named in honor of Susan's grandmother, who inspired her to work on behalf of animals, launched in November 2007 with the initial goal of making 100 cage comforters for New York City's city-run animal shelters. Thirty volunteers showed up at the first sewing party and finished forty-five comforters. Over the next year, the group made almost 500 more, from kitten-size comforters to beds big enough for the many pit bulls and German shepherd mixes picked up by New York's Animal Care and Control Agency. The comforters are quick and easy to make: two pieces of fabric are sewn together, pillowcase style, stuffed with batting, stitched up, and quilted to keep the batting from shifting around.

The little quilts help animals in shelters in two ways. They provide physical comfort, which reduces stress, making the animals less likely to fall ill and more likely to be adopted. And it also seems that they make it easier for humans to fall in love with the animals. "When people come to the shelter to adopt an animal," Krysta explains, "and they see it frantic in a bare metal cage, it's hard for them to see this animal in their life. But when they see a little dog curled up on a little comforter, they can picture it more—they can make a connection with the animal."

Many animal shelters across the country accept donated cage comforters. At smaller shelters, adopted dogs and cats often take their comforters with them to their new homes; having something that smells familiar can help with the transition. But because turnover is so high at New York City's shelters, the comforters are washed and reused by lots of animals. Krysta picks up free fabric at a warehouse run by Material for the Arts, an organization that provides all kinds of art materials to nonprofits. She chooses denim and upholstery-weight fabric donated by clothing companies and design houses, because regular cottons aren't sturdy enough to withstand claws, teeth, and frequent washings.

The volunteer quilters who attend Mother's Comfort gatherings have one thing in common: their commitment to animals. "Everyone is inspired to come because of their love for animals," Krysta says. "While they're sewing and cutting and stuffing these comforters, people talk about their companion animals and their work helping animals. There's definitely a sense of community. Before you know it, four hours are over. It's such an amazing sense of accomplishment to stack all these beautiful comforters up. And it's so exciting to take them over to the shelter and see them go to the animals." ✳

HOW YOU CAN HELP

Call your local shelter and offer
to make cage comforters
(see the pattern on page 30).
Be sure to ask what sizes are most
needed and how they'd like you to stuff
the comforters. Some shelters
don't allow polyester batting, as
it can be easily shredded by
an anxious animal.

If you live in New York City, attend a
Mother's Comfort sewing party. Go to
www.rational-animal.org/MothersComfort
for a list of upcoming dates.

Make a cage comforter and send it to
New York Animal Care and Control at:
Mayor's Alliance for NYC's Animals
440 Ninth Avenue
8th floor, Suite 9
New York, NY 10001.

Learn more at
www.animalalliancenyc.org/supportus/
comforters.htm.

Cage Comforter

ADAPTED FROM A PATTERN CREATED BY THE MOTHER'S COMFORT PROJECT

These simple dog and cat beds make metal cages a little more comfortable and increase homeless animals' odds of being adopted. The Mother's Comfort group suggests using recycled or leftover upholstery-weight cotton. Check with your local animal shelter to find out what kind of batting they prefer since some shelters won't accept cage quilts made with polyester batting.

FINISHED SIZE

Small: 13 inches x 19 inches
Medium: 17 inches x 25 inches
Large: 23 inches x 35 inches

WHAT YOU'LL NEED

Sturdy cotton (preferably upholstery weight) in 2 contrasting colors: 2 fat quarters (for small comforter); 1/2 yard each of 36-inch-wide cotton (for medium comforter); 3/4 yard each of 36-inch-wide cotton (for large comforter)

Thick batting (or 2-3 layers of recycled fleece or towels), in dimensions called for in sewing instructions for each comforter size

Safety pins

Knitting needle or chopstick

Matching cotton thread

SEWING INSTRUCTIONS

Small comforter (for cats and small dogs)

1. Cut two 14-inch x 20-inch rectangles of fabric for the top and bottom of the comforter.

2. Cut a 13½-inch x 19½-inch piece of batting.

3. Place the comforter top, right side up, on a table or on the floor. Align the comforter bottom, wrong side up, on top of the comforter top. Center the batting atop the two fabric pieces, and use safety pins to "baste" the three layers together.

4. Sew around three sides of the layered "sandwich" with a 3/8-inch seam, just catching the edge of the batting.

5. Remove the safety pins, and turn the comforter right side out, using a knitting needle or chopstick to push out the corners fully. Smooth out the batting.

   At the open edge, fold the top fabric over the batting to cover it, and then fold the bottom fabric to align with the covered edge; and pin the folded edges in place. Edge-stitch (see page 130) these folded edges closed.

6. Using tailor's chalk, mark diagonal lines between the comforter's opposite corners. Then mark a horizontal line and a vertical line, each running from edge to edge through the center of the X formed by the diagonal lines (see Diagram A). Stitch along these marked lines, lockstitching or backstitching (see page 130) at the beginning and end of each seam to secure it.

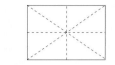
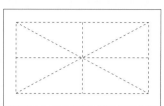

Medium comforter
(for medium-size dogs)

Cut two 18-inch x 26-inch rectangles for the top and bottom of the comforter. Cut the batting ½ inch smaller than the rectangles' dimensions. Then follow steps 3-6 above to construct the comforter.

Large comforter *(for large dogs)*

Cut two 24-inch x 36-inch rectangles for the top and bottom of the comforter. Cut the batting ½ inch smaller than the rectangles' dimensions. Follow steps 3-5 above to begin constructing the comforter. Then stitch a rectangle 3 inches in from the edge of the comforter (see Diagram B). Finally follow the beginning of step 6 to stitch diagonal, vertical, and horizontal lines within the stitched rectangle.

Wartime Quilting

Few things rouse the volunteer spirit among quilters like wars. When President Abraham Lincoln called up the militias at the beginning of the Civil War in 1861, the government was unprepared to outfit or provide basic bedding for its new Union Army. Across the North, women sprang into action. Immediately, 20,000 newly formed soldiers' aid societies—as well as the tightly organized and highly effective U.S. Sanitary Commission, which laid the foundation for the American Red Cross—got to work.

Together, Union women produced enormous numbers of uniforms, socks, and bandages for their soldiers—and at least a quarter-million quilts. Southern women stitched for their soldiers as well, although their efforts were hampered by severe supply shortages. Once they had cut up nearly every curtain and bedspread in the Confederacy, they began weaving their own fabric and spinning their own thread.

In later wars, the U.S. military no longer needed to rely on civilian seamstresses to supply the troops, but the tradition of wartime quilting continued. During World War I, signature quilts were made to raise funds for the American Red Cross, and women were urged to make quilts to be used on the home front, in order to "save the blankets for the boys over there." Few quilts were made for soldiers in World War II, but tens of thousands were sent to refugees in war-ravaged Europe. And more recently, during the 1991 Gulf War, women made quilts mainly to express their support for or opposition to the invasion.

The most recent wars in Afghanistan and Iraq have directly affected a much smaller percentage of the American population than earlier conflicts, but many American quilters still feel called to action. They fall on both sides of the political divide, but when they see suffering, grief, or injustice, they are often moved to do something about it, however small and symbolic. They are often moved, in other words, to quilt.

Of the wartime quilters in this chapter, some quilt in protest. Others quilt to bring comfort to soldiers and their families. But they all honor the men and women who have fought, and they bring an abiding sense of duty and patriotism to their wartime quilting efforts. The projects included reflect this sentiment; they are not difficult, but are a bit more time-consuming than those in other chapters. These quilts, the sacrifices they honor and the survivors they touch, deserve a little extra care and time.

Home of the Brave Quilts

During the Civil War, many of the contributions of Northern women were coordinated by the United States Sanitary Commission, a private relief agency created to support and supply Northern troops and to oversee the conditions in military hospitals. Modeled on a British organization that did similar work during the Crimean War, the U.S. Sanitary Commission laid the foundation for the American Red Cross. Of the more than 125,000 quilts made by women associated with the Sanitary Commission, only six remain. (Most were worn out or destroyed in the war, or wrapped around fallen soldiers and buried on the battlefield.) One of the six surviving quilts hangs at the Lincoln Shrine at the public library in Redlands, California, not far from the home of Don Beld, a quilter and amateur quilt historian. Inspired by this quilt, Don founded Home of the Brave Quilts, a grassroots movement of quilters who sew quilts for the families of American servicemen and -women who have lost their lives in Iraq and Afghanistan.

Don has made many memorial quilts over the years. In the early 1990s, while his son was dying of AIDS, Don spent many long hours at his bedside, occupying his hands by doing cross-stitch. He'd taken up the hobby almost twenty years earlier as a way to relieve stress, inspired by Rosey Grier, a former defensive tackle for the New York Giants and the Los Angeles Rams who famously enjoyed needlepoint and macramé and published a book called *Needlepoint for Men*.

After his son died, though, Don found cross-stitching too painful. He stitched a panel in memory of his son for the AIDS quilt (see page 108), the massive fabric memorial that names tens of thousands of victims of the disease, and then he gave up the craft altogether. He didn't want to quit needlework entirely, though, so he took a quilting class, in which he learned to piece and quilt by hand.

In 1998, Don joined the Citrus Belt Quilters in Redlands, California. In 2004, the guild decided to make quilts for local families who had lost loved ones in Iraq and Afghanistan, and Don volunteered to organize the project. He liked the idea of copying the Lincoln Shrine quilt because local families could visit the original. Home of the Brave Quilts grew organically out of those small beginnings until it became a national grassroots movement.

Home of the Brave quilters pattern their quilts after those made by Sanitary Commission volunteers; most are replicas of the "album block" quilt on display at the Lincoln Shrine. The album block, a square containing a diagonal cross with a small square of muslin at its center, was a popular pattern in the years leading up to the Civil War. When a woman married or moved away, her friends often made an album block or other "signature" quilt for her; they signed the center pieces of the blocks so that she wouldn't forget them. Sanitary Commission quilters often signed the white center pieces of the blocks, and today, some Home of the Brave quilters ask friends and family to sign the quilts they make as an extra show of support for the grieving families.

Home of the Brave takes no stand on the wars in Iraq and Afghanistan. "It's not an issue of supporting the wars," Don says. "It's not even an issue of supporting the troops. It's a personal belief of mine that when someone sacrifices their life in the service of our country, we cannot do enough to honor them. So the idea is to honor these fallen heroes. The thing that people tend to forget is that not only did they lose their lives, but their families have to live with the sacrifice for the rest of their lives."

It can be difficult to locate the families of those killed in action, because the military protects their addresses and other information. In the first few years, Home of the Brave coordinators had to do quite a bit of detective work, calling funeral homes and schools listed in soldiers' obituaries, for example. Over the years, the group built enough credibility to work directly with the Department of Defense, which now shares contact information for the next of kin of any soldiers who signed releases. For the others, Don says, "You can find anyone if you try hard enough."

It took Don a year and a half to find the family of Billy Gomez, a twenty-five-year-old Army medic killed by an IED (improvised explosive device) in Afghanistan in 2004. When he finally spoke to Billy's mother, she asked if he would put her other sons' names on the quilt as well. She told Don that Billy had been a triplet; one of his brothers was serving in Iraq at the time, and the other was about to be deployed. "I just hope we never have to make her another quilt," Don says.

WARMING THE TROOPS

QUILTS	30,197
BLANKETS	13,500
SHEETS	42,945
PILLOWS	35,877
PILLOW-TICKS	2,269
BED-TICKS	11,716

CIVIL WAR FUNDRAISING

In addition to sewing and collecting supplies, the women of the U.S. Sanitary Commission auctioned elaborate quilts and other crafts at fund-raising fairs. By the end of the war, the value of their contributions to the war effort equaled $25 million. In a speech at the Washington, D.C., Sanitary Fair in 1864, President Abraham Lincoln said:

In this extraordinary war, extraordinary developments have manifested themselves, such as have not been seen in former wars; and amongst these manifestations nothing has been more remarkable than these fairs for the relief of suffering soldiers and their families. And the chief agents in these fairs are the women of America...I have never studied the art of paying compliments to women; but I must say, that if all that has been said by orators and poets since the creation of the world in praise of women were applied to the women of America, it would not do them justice for their conduct during this war...God bless the women of America.

When possible, Home of the Brave tries to give quilts to all of the closest relatives of each soldier. That can mean several quilts for a single family: one for the spouse, one for each child, and another for the parents—two if they're separated or divorced. To date, that adds up to 2,300 Home of the Brave quilts made for 2,050 families.

Like the Sanitary Commission quilts of the Civil War era, which were designed to fit on a narrow hospital cot, Home of the Brave quilts are long and narrow in shape. Don describes them as "big enough to be useful" now as well, pointing out that they fit perfectly over a child's twin bed, offering tangible comfort to children who have lost a parent in one of the wars. Mothers who have lost sons or daughters have often told Don that they wrap themselves in their quilts when they feel lonely.

Because it isn't registered as a nonprofit organization, Home of the Brave takes no donations and relies entirely on word of mouth and free publicity to recruit volunteers. Connections among quilters and quilting guilds, articles in national quilting magazines, and the group's website have helped news about the project spread beyond California. While Don no longer takes an active role in the movement— a national coordinator, Sandi Carstensen, who lives in Iowa, has taken charge of Home of the Brave's website, its relationships with the media, and its database of casualties—his original intentions still fuel the organization.

Don feels strongly that no matter how large the group grows, it should remain an informal effort. He wants each quilt to be a gift from an individual quilter to a particular family. Quilters buy their own fabric, and volunteer coordinators in each state keep track of casualties, find the families, and deliver the quilts.

Some volunteers are incredibly prolific. In a few small states, a single quilter makes quilts for all the lost soldiers' families in the state; in others, many guilds and quilting groups contribute. A woman in California whose son, stationed at Fort Bragg, North Carolina, is the highest noncommissioned officer in the Army, has made a quilt for every soldier lost from her son's Stryker brigade. As soon as she had finished all of those, she singlehandedly took on all of Home of the Brave's work in Orange County. That level of dedication isn't mandatory, however. "If you only make one quilt," Don says, "that's one family that will have been honored. It's better to make one quilt than none at all."

Home of the Brave album quilts also hang in Capitol and other state buildings in five states. Each quilt bears the names of the state's casualties on its blocks. When Don hand-pieced California's state quilt, he included 100 blocks, each with space for four names. At the time, 240 Californians had died in Iraq and Afghanistan. Five years into the Iraq War, that number had more than doubled. The original quilt is full, and Don has had to make three side panels, each with room for forty more names. "It's really a comment about the war," Don says. "The quilt was 110 inches square, and there wasn't enough room for the names."

Don sees Home of the Brave's work as part of a massive community service movement inseparable from its historic roots. "The longest running nonreligious philanthropic charitable movement in the history of the world is the community service quilts of America's quilters," he says. "And yet it's so unsung. We're talking tens of millions of quilts. No one gets credit for it, no one talks about it, and it all traces back to the Sanitary Commission." ✳

HOW YOU CAN HELP

Make individual blocks, a quilt top, or a complete album quilt (see the pattern on page 38) for Home of the Brave. Hand-quilted, machine-quilted, and tied quilts are accepted. (The original Sanitary Commission quilts were either tied or quilted with simple geometric patterns.)

Home of the Brave Quilts asks volunteers to use high-quality quilting fabric appropriate for the Civil War period— blues, reds, browns, and tans. Windham Fabrics (www.windhamfabrics.com) makes a great line of Civil War reproduction fabrics.

If you ask people to sign the muslin center square of the album blocks, first iron a piece of freezer paper to the back of the square. Home of the Brave recommends using a Sakura Micron Pigma or a Zig Millenium pen (available at many craft supply stores)— any other pen may bleed when the quilt gets wet. Using a dry iron, press from the front to set the signatures, then peel off the freezer paper.

Contact your state coordinator or the national coordinator to find out where to send your donations. Find contact information at www.homeofthebravequilts.com.

Civil War Album Quilt

ADAPTED FROM THE HOME OF THE BRAVE PATTERN

The pattern for this quilt comes from a Civil War album block quilt used by a Union soldier—the original hangs at the Lincoln Shrine in Redlands, California. Women in the North made more than a quarter-million quilts like this one for the troops. Its long, narrow shape was intended to fit the cots used in field hospitals. I've widened and shortened the quilt by a few inches to make it more suited to snuggling under on the sofa. If you'd rather stick to the original dimensions (48 inches x 84 inches), as most Home of the Brave volunteers do, simply cut the side borders 3½ inches deep and the top and bottom borders 7 inches deep.

FINISHED SIZE

52 inches x 78 inches

WHAT YOU'LL NEED

15 fat quarters (see page 131) in various cotton Civil War reproduction prints (for blocks)

2⅝-inch x 40-inch strip of unbleached muslin (for blocks)

1¾ yards of 44-inch-wide Civil War reproduction print (for sashing and borders)

3½-inch x 28-inch strip of contrasting cotton Civil War reproduction print (for cornerstones)

3 yards of 44-inch-wide cotton Civil War reproduction print (for backing)

½ yard of 44-inch-wide cotton Civil War reproduction print (for binding)

Matching cotton thread

12½-inch-square quilter's ruler (optional)

SEWING INSTRUCTIONS

1. Cut an 11-inch square from one fat quarter. Next cut the square diagonally from one corner to the opposite corner, forming two triangles. Then cut each triangle into two triangles by cutting a perpendicular line from the center of the longest side to the opposite corner (see Diagram A on page 41).

2. Cut four 2⅝-inch x 9-inch strips from a contrasting fat quarter.

3. Cut one 2⅝-inch square from the muslin.

4. With one triangle laid right side up, carefully lay one cut strip, right side down on one of the triangle's short sides, matching the strip's end with the triangle's right angle. Be careful as you're positioning the triangle and strip not to stretch the triangle's bias-cut edges. (Note that the strip will be longer than the triangle's short side, but you'll trim this later.) Sew the aligned edges of the strip and triangle with a ¼-inch seam. (Sewing with the strip on top will help prevent the triangle's bias edge from stretching; note, too, that you'll use a ¼-inch seam for all the steps below.) Press the seam allowances together toward the strip.

5. Turn the sewn strip/triangle right side up, and position a second triangle, right side down, on the strip, matching the strip's end with the triangle's right angle and using a pin or two to hold the strip and new triangle in position. With the strip on top, sew the aligned edges together. Press the seam allowances together toward the strip.

6. Repeat steps 4-5 to join the other two triangles to a second cut strip.

7. With right sides together and the edges aligned, sew the short edges of the two remaining strips to opposite sides of the muslin square, creating a long strip of fabric. Press the seam allowances together toward the darker fabric.

8. With one pieced triangle unit right side up, place the long strip, right side down, on top of the traingle's long edge, aligning the edges and carefully matching the seams at the center square (see Diagram B). Sew the long strip and triangle unit together, and press the seams together toward the darker fabric. Repeat this process to join the strip to the second pieced triangle unit (see Diagram C).

9. Now trim the block to 12½ inches square, using a ruler (a 12½-inch square ruler is ideal) and aligning the ruler's markings with the corners of the central square (see Diagram D). Alternatively, use your cutting mat as a guide for squaring up and trimming the block.

10. Repeat steps 1-9 until you have 15 pieced blocks.

11. Cut twenty-two 3½-inch x 12½-inch strips from your sashing fabric.

12. Cut eight 3½-inch squares from the cornerstone fabric for the cornerstones.

13. Arrange your blocks on the floor in rows of three across and five down. Begin joining the blocks by sewing each horizontal row together: With right sides together and the edges aligned, sew one sashing strip to one side of the first block. Then sew the sashing's other long edge to the opposite side of the second block. Finally sew another sashing strip to the opposite side of the second block and to one side of the third block. Then press all the seam allowances toward the sashing strips.

14. Repeat step 13 with each of the four remaining horizontal rows of blocks.

15. To create the long sashing strips to sew between each horizontal row, sew together the following, with right sides together and the edges aligned: one 12½-inch strip, one cornerstone, one 12½-inch strip, one cornerstone, and one 12½-inch strip.

16. Repeat step 15 three more times.

17. Sew these horizontal sashing strips to the bottom edge of each of the first four rows, pressing the seam allowances toward the sashing strip.

  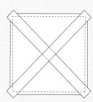

18. Sew the five rows together, matching the cornerstone seams to the edges of the blocks.

19. To create the wide borders that you'll attach to the sides of the quilt, cut four 5½-inch-deep, selvedge-to-selvedge strips from your sashing/border fabric, and then cut off the selvedges at each end of these strips.

    With right sides together and the edges aligned, sew together the short ends of two of the strips to create one long border strip. Repeat the process with the other two strips. Finally, with right sides together and the edges aligned, sew one border strip to one long edge of the quilt, and trim any excess on the ends. Repeat the process to join a border strip to the other long edge of the quilt.

20. To create the border strips for the top and bottom of the quilt, cut three 3½-inch-deep, selvedge-to-selvedge strips from the border fabric. Cut one strip in half, and sew each short 3½-inch strip to each long strip. Then sew one border strip to the top and one to the bottom of the quilt top, and trim any excess.

21. Layer the quilt top, batting, and backing to make a quilt sandwich, and pin it in place (see page 128).

22. Beginning in the middle of the quilt and working outward, machine-quilt using any pattern your choose. Allover meander-quilting (see page 130) is a good choice for this quilt.

23. Create a traditional binding for the quilt following the directions on page 129.

Seattle Veterans' Quilts

Betsy Shapiro began working as a psychiatric nurse at the Seattle Veterans Administration Hospital in 1979, five years after the Vietnam War ended. For most of her twenty-four years there, she took care of patients who suffered from post-traumatic stress disorder (PTSD), substance abuse, and in many cases, both. Most were Vietnam combat veterans, but she also worked with vets from World War II and Korea, as well as a few from Grenada and the 1991 Gulf War.

In the years after Vietnam, it seemed to Betsy that few people outside the medical profession knew much about PTSD, a psychological condition that can result from extremely disturbing experiences and causes nightmares, flashbacks, severe anxiety, and emotional problems. "This is a dreadful, dreadful illness that causes so much sadness, and people need to know about it," she says. In the early 1990s, she learned about the AIDS quilt (see page 108), an epic project made from panels commemorating an individual death, which added up to a monumental and devastating proof of the cost of the disease. The AIDS quilt raised awareness effectively; perhaps, she thought, a PTSD quilt could do the same.

Betsy and her colleagues had also noticed that the help and comfort veterans gave each other was often the most effective. Sometimes when she counseled patients, she says, "they would challenge me and say, 'How can you know? You weren't there.' And it was true—I wasn't there. The other veterans knew the pain. They let them know they weren't alone, that there were others who had experienced things similar to their experiences." That sense of being understood is absolutely crucial to veterans suffering from PTSD. Betsy had been looking for a way for veterans to comfort those admitted to the hospital after them, and quilts, she knew, were almost universally comforting.

She gathered a small group of patients and gave each one a six-inch square of khaki fabric and a fistful of markers. She asked the men to draw or write something on the fabric that would show future patients that somebody understood their feelings. Some of the veterans were "pretty snarly about it" at first, protesting that they weren't artists. But they all ended up participating, and Betsy repeated the project with a new group of veterans every month for more than a decade. No one ever refused to contribute a square. Many drew their unit or battalion insignias, or helicopters, tanks, or battleships. Some drew disturbing images—a helmeted medic crying blood, for example—and on occasion a vet insulted the generals who commanded operations during the Vietnam War. Betsy never put any limits on what they could draw or write.

Betsy didn't have any experience quilting, so when she'd accumulated the first forty-five squares, she put an ad in a quilting magazine, looking for someone to sew the blocks together into a quilt. The widow of a World War II veteran volunteered. After that, a nurse who had rotated through the Seattle VA's PTSD ward as a student took over the quilting. When she tried sewing sashing—narrow bands of fabric—between the squares, the vets protested; they wanted their blocks to touch each other.

By the time Betsy retired in 2003, ten quilts hung on the walls of the PTSD ward. When veterans were admitted, it was often after resisting treatment for a long time. The quilts, Betsy says, confirmed that they had arrived at the right place, a place where people understood the never-ending horror of their experiences during the war. The veterans never said much, but they spent a long time looking at the quilts and often, especially when they spotted their own unit symbols, touched the fabric.

The hospital's recreational therapist, Todd Thomas, took over the quilt project after Betsy retired. There are fewer Vietnam vets these days, but they have been replaced by younger men and women who have served in Iraq and Afghanistan. They come with a different experience of war and new problems rarely seen during earlier wars—like traumatic brain injuries sustained during explosions that would have killed soldiers wearing Vietnam-era body armor. But many of the symptoms for which they're admitted to the PTSD ward—the crippling anxiety, for example—are not terribly different from those suffered by the veterans who preceded them. The PTSD quilts tell all of their stories— past and ever-present. ✳

> 66
>
> **The love of our neighbor in all its fullness simply means being able to say to him, 'What are you going through?'**
>
> 99
>
> SIMONE WEIL

To the Top and Quilts of Valor

Private First Class Evan O'Neill was killed in action in Shkin, Afghanistan, on September 29, 2003. He was nineteen years old. On the day Evan died, his mother's best friend, Bev True, drove down to Massachusetts from Maine to stay with the O'Neills. Evan's mother, Barbara, and Bev were both quilters; they'd met ten years earlier in an online quilting group. Barbara remembers, "I kept saying to her, 'What am I going to do? This was my only son. What am I going to do?' She said, 'We'll figure out what to do. We'll find something to do.'"

A couple of days later, the executive director of the Veterans Northeast Outreach Center in Haverhill, Massachusetts, where the O'Neills lived, called to say that they were planning to build a new veterans' residence, and that they wanted to name the building after Evan. Bev immediately recognized the something-to-do Barbara needed: Together, they would make quilts for these local veterans. "When there's a tragedy," Barbara says, "you do what you need to do, and then you recruit other people to help you." She started an online quilting group named To the Top, after the motto of Evan's regiment, the 1st Battalion, 87th Infantry of the 10th Mountain Division.

When the new occupants of the Evan W. O'Neill Memorial Hall moved in, Barbara and Bev delivered a quilt to each of them. That turned out to be just the beginning: they went on to give over 500 quilts to veterans living in long-term shelters and veterans' residences across Massachusetts and southern New Hampshire.

The year Evan was killed, Nat Roberts, a military policeman from Delaware, was deployed to Iraq. His mother, Catherine, a former nurse-midwife, vowed to keep herself extremely busy in order to stay sane while he was away. Like Barbara O'Neill, Catherine Roberts was a longtime quilter. She searched on the Internet to see if any groups were making quilts for soldiers wounded in combat. When she couldn't find one, she started the Quilts of Valor Foundation, "to recruit wartime quilters to make wartime quilts." Since then, with the help of military chaplains, the organization has given more than 18,000 quilts to wounded soldiers and marines. Catherine's goal is to give quilts to all wounded service members and veterans from the wars in Iraq and Afghanistan, whether their wounds are physical or psychological. And she interprets that liberally. "Anyone who has had their boots in the sandbox is affected," she says.

Though they operate at different scales—To the Top is still primarily a local effort, while Quilts of Valor has become a national organization with 172 dedicated quilting groups in 46 states, as well as hundreds of individual volunteers—both organizations emphasize that their quilts are intended not only to comfort but also to honor the veterans and active-duty troops who receive them.

Most To the Top quilts go to Vietnam vets, but veterans of World War II, the Korean War, the Gulf War, and the current wars in Afghanistan and Iraq have also received quilts. Bev and Barbara have made about half of the quilts themselves. The rest have been made by more than 100 volunteers from across the United States and as far away as Iceland, nearly all of whom were moved to contribute after visiting To the Top's online community at www.neverforgetthefallen.org. Often, volunteers send single blocks that Barbara pieces together into quilt tops that she then sends to Bev in Maine to be quilted on her professional long-arm quilting machine. "We'll take one block, twenty blocks, a million blocks. We're not picky," Barbara says.

Quilts of Valor's quilt-making process is much more complex. Volunteers who sign up as "quilt-toppers" piece lap-size or twin-size quilt tops in any pattern they choose. (Most are patriotic designs in red, white, and blue with stars and stripes, but that's not a requirement.) Catherine asks her volunteers to make quilts they'd want to give their own children, using the best fabric they can afford. These quilts should last for generations, she says, but they're meant to be used, not packed away as heirlooms. When she pieces quilts for soldiers herself, she chooses patterns that are a little more challenging as an extra way of honoring the recipients.

Quilt-toppers are matched with professional quilters who squeeze their volunteer work for Quilts of Valor in between their paying jobs. Each volunteer keeps a journal about the experience of making a quilt—usually in the form of a collection of letters to the recipient—and these are given to wounded soldiers along with the quilts. Soldiers appreciate them, Catherine says, almost as much as the quilts themselves. In a thank-you note, a wounded sergeant in West Virginia wrote, "What really moved me about the quilt was the personal touch. My quilt isn't another military medal to be placed in a box and sat on a shelf, but something that was given to me by a woman I may never have the pleasure

> **"**
>
> **My son is in the army. Whoever is made warm by this quilt, which I have worked on for six days and most of six nights, let him remember his mother's love."**
>
> **"**
>
> *A note pinned to a quilt donated to the Sanitary Commission during the Civil War*

of meeting, just because she cared…Along with physical injuries, I also suffer from PTSD [post-traumatic stress disorder]. It's the love and warmth that went into every stitch of the quilt that brings me comfort."

A social worker Catherine knows who specializes in treating post-traumatic stress disorder says that a stranger's acknowledgment of the veteran's service can sometimes be the first step in healing. "So the quilt," Catherine says, "which is something tangible and beautiful, can start this. I'm not saying it's a panacea for PTSD, but it's a start. It says, Yes, I served, and yes, someone appreciates what I did."

Quilts of Valor's strongest endorsement comes from Al Lind, a World War II veteran and former prisoner of war who has made 110 Quilts of Valor. In a video recorded and posted on YouTube to help the group recruit volunteers, Al, sitting at his sewing machine covered with military decals, urges other retired men to become wartime quilters: "Anybody could sit down with a sewing machine and start sewing Quilts of Valor for these veterans that are coming back wounded and all tore up and everything," he says. "They would appreciate very much getting these quilts and realizing that people do care for what they're doing and for what they have done. I know that they appreciate getting them too because I've seen pictures of some of them receiving some of my quilts. And I think it's a great honor to do this, so get off your duff and get started."

The act of stitching concern and gratitude into wartime quilts has a profound effect on their makers, as well as on their recipients. It helps Barbara cope with her grief. "To me, if I'm sewing, if I'm making a vet's quilt, I'm connecting with my son," she says. "That has always been a big help." And according to Catherine, the experience of making Quilts of Valor, as well as writing to the wounded soldiers who will receive them, gives quilters who don't have loved ones serving in the military some insight into the terrible—and unevenly distributed—cost of war. ✳

TO THE TOP

To the Top asks volunteers to make a square, a top,
or a whole quilt to donate to veterans' residences.

For more information on the To the Top Quilt Project and
to find out where to send partial or completed quilts,
visit **www.neverforgetthefallen.org**.

Join the To the Top Yahoo Group at
www.groups.yahoo.com/group/TotheTopProject.

QUILTS OF VALOR

Quilts of Valor requests quilt tops at least 50 inches x 60 inches
and no larger than 72 inches x 90 inches, made using
high-quality 100-percent cotton fabric and a backing at least
4 inches larger than the quilt top on all sides.

Quilts of Valor encourages volunteers to give finished quilts to
wounded soldiers in their own communities. To do so, call the nearest
Vet Center or Veteran's Administration Medical Center,
which can be found at **www.va.gov**.

To be paired with a volunteer quilter who will
machine quilt your top, or to donate
fabric, fund-raise, or join a local Quilts of Valor group,
go to **www.qovf.org**.

Sawtooth Star Quilt

When making quilts for wounded soldiers, many Quilts of Valor volunteers choose patterns that include stars and stripes. This pattern isn't difficult, but it requires a lot of detailed piecing, so it takes time. Don't worry if the points of your stars aren't perfect; they will still be beautiful.

FINISHED SIZE
67 inches x 88 inches

WHAT YOU'LL NEED
1 yard each of 44-inch-wide quilting cotton in four shades of blue (for stars)

5¾ yards of 44-inch-wide, grey quilting cotton (for quilt-block backgrounds, sashing, borders, and binding)

6 yards of 44-inch-wide, grey or blue quilting cotton (for backing)

Twin-sized (93 inches x 72 inches) cotton batting

Matching grey cotton thread

SEWING INSTRUCTIONS

1. For the centers of the stars, cut two 3½-inch-deep, selvedge-to-selvedge strips of each of the four blue fabrics. Cut each strip into twelve 3½-inch squares. You will need 22 squares in each fabric (88 squares total) and will have two extra squares of each fabric (8 extra squares).

2. For the star points, cut nine 2-inch selvedge-to-selvedge strips of each blue fabric. Cut each of these into twenty 2-inch squares. You'll need 176 squares in each of the four fabrics (704 squares total) and will have four extra squares of each fabric (16 extra squares).

3. For the background of the blocks, cut eighteen 3½-inch selvedge-to-selvedge strips of the grey background fabric. Trim 1 inch off each end of the strips to remove the selvedges; then re-cut these strips every 2 inches to create twenty 2-inch x 3½-inch rectangles (360 rectangles total). You'll need 352 rectangles and will have 8 extras.

4. For the corners of the blocks, cut eighteen 2-inch selvedge-to-selvedge strips of the grey background fabric. Trim 1 inch off each end of the strips to remove the selvedges; then cut each of these strips into twenty 2-inch squares (360 squares total). You'll need 352 squares and have 8 extras.

5. For the sashing between the blocks, cut six 6½-inch-deep selvedge-to-selvedge strips of the grey background fabric. Trim 1 inch off each end of the strips to remove the selvedges; then cut these strips every 1½ inches to create twenty-seven 6½-inch x 1½-inch strips (162 strips total). You'll need 157 sashing strips and will have five extras.

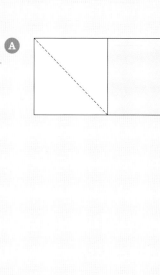

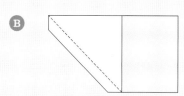

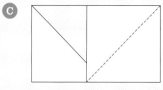

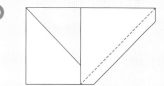

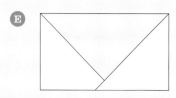

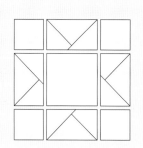

6. For the cornerstones that you'll sew to the sashing strips, cut three 1½-inch-deep, selvedge-to-selvedge strips of the grey background fabric. Trim 1 inch off each end of the strips to remove the selvedges; then cut each strip into twenty-seven 1½-inch squares (81 squares). You'll need 70 squares and will have 11 extras.

7. Each star contains four Flying Geese triangles. To make each set of four triangles, draw a diagonal corner-to-corner line with a chalk marker across the wrong side of each of eight matching 2-inch blue squares. With right sides together, lay one square on top of one end of one grey 2-inch x 3½-inch rectangle. Sew along the marked line through both fabric layers (see Diagram A).

Cut both fabrics ¼ inch away from this seam (see Diagram B). Then press open the joined triangle, pressing the seam allowances toward the grey fabric.

8. Place another 2-inch square, right side down, on the other end of the 3½-inch x 2-inch rectangle. Sew along the marked line (see Diagram C). Cut ¼ inch away from the sewn line (see Diagram D). Press the blue triangle open (see Diagram E).

Repeat the process three times to make three more Flying Geese triangles.

9. Piece together four corner squares, four Flying Geese triangles, and one center square to form a star (see Diagram F), joining each of the pieces with a ¼-inch seam and with right sides together and the edges aligned (note that, for all the seaming in the steps below, you should also use a ¼-inch seam). Take extra care as you reach the points of the triangles to make sure your seam hits each point as accurately as possible.

10. Repeat steps 7-9 until you have sewn 88 stars.

11. To prepare the sashing, sew one cornerstone to one short end of one 6½-inch strip. Press the seam allowances toward the cornerstone. Repeat this step with the remaining 69 cornerstones.

   With right sides together, sew a 6½-inch sashing strip to one side of one star. Press the seam allowances toward the star. Repeat this step with all but 11 of the remaining stars.

12. On the floor, arrange the 77 star-and-sashing blocks you created in step 11 into eleven rows of seven blocks with the sashing strip on the right of each block. Add one star without a sashing strip to the right end of each row. Move the blocks around until you are happy with the distribution of blues, always keeping a star without a sashing strip on the right end of each row.

13. Sew each row together, pressing the seam allowances toward the sashing strips.

14. Create a long sashing strip to go between the rows by sewing the short end of a 6½-inch strip to a cornerstone (with right sides together), followed by another sashing strip, another cornerstone, and so on, until you have sewn eight strips with seven cornerstones between them. Press the seam allowances together toward the sashing strips. Repeat to create nine more long sashing strips.

15. Sew a long sashing strip to the bottom of each star row, except the eleventh star row at the bottom of the quilt. As you sew, match every seam, pinching the two layers of fabric together at each intersection to keep the seams aligned until they reach your sewing machine's presser foot.

16. Sew the bottom of each long sashing strip to the top of each star row to complete the quilt top, again matching every seam.

17. To make the borders, cut eight 6½-inch-deep, selvedge-to-selvedge strips from the grey background fabric, and trim away the selvedge edges. Sew pairs of these strips together end to end, pressing the seam allowances to one side, to make four long border strips. Sew a border strip to each long side of the quilt top, and press the seam allowances toward the borders. Trim the ends of the strips even with the edges of the quilt top. Then sew the remaining border strips to the top and bottom of the quilt top, again pressing the seam allowances toward the borders, and trimming the ends of the border strips.

18. Cut the backing fabric into two pieces, each 3 yards long, trimming the selvedge edges. Sew the two backing pieces together along one long side and press the seam allowances to one side.

19. Make a quilt sandwich and pin it in place (see page 128).

20. Meander-quilt (see page 130) between the stars, avoiding quilting over the stars themselves.

21. Bind the quilt following the directions for making a traditional binding on page 129.

Quilts Over Kosovo

In late March 1999, NATO forces began air strikes against Slobodan Milosevic's Serbian forces, which retaliated by stepping up their efforts to empty Kosovo of all ethnic Albanians. In the two weeks after the bombing began, more than 375,000 refugees fled across the borders of Albania and Macedonia. Relief agencies were unprepared to handle a crisis of that magnitude, and it didn't help that the weather was terribly cold and rainy.

Six thousand miles away, in Boise, Idaho, journalist and quilter Jill Kuraitis watched footage of refugees marching through mud and rain on the television news. "The image that sent me over the edge was an old woman pushing an older old woman in a handcart. My mother was ill at the time, and I was very close to her. I saw these two old ladies and thought, 'That is somebody's mother, somebody's mother-in-law, somebody's grandmother.' And I just cried. I couldn't help myself." After enduring what looked to Jill like a "death march," the refugees arrived at an enormous camp that didn't appear much better: "It looked like hell on earth, acres and acres of miserable humanity in the mud and the rain."

The sight of so many cold refugees inspired Jill to organize as many quilters as she could to make quilts to send to the camps. She envisioned the quilts not just as bedding, but shelter; when her kids were small, they'd hung big quilts over the clothesline in the backyard and played at camping beneath them, and that image stuck in her mind. After consulting with refugee organizations, she devised specific instructions to make the quilts most useful. They had to be big—ideally at least full-size, filled with quick-drying polyester or synthetic fleece, and closely quilted for durability. And despite the urgency, she wanted volunteers to piece the quilts with as much attention to design and detail as they would if they were making them for their own families.

Jill e-mailed all the quilters she knew, asking them to contribute quilts and also to forward her request to other quilters. Within two days she was receiving thirty e-mails an hour from all over the United States and a handful of other countries. She started a website called Quilts Over Kosovo and hooked up with a relief organization willing and able to deliver the quilts to the camps. In just two weeks, 3,000 quilts were ready to be shipped.

Within a month, Jill began spotting quilts she recognized in news footage of the refugee camps. Just as she'd imagined, they were being used as colorful tents.

Quilts Over Kosovo produced about 10,000 quilts for the refugees. After about six months, the project wound down, as the immediate crisis in Kosovo passed and Jill and the other quilters turned their attention to quilting for people affected by other tragedies. In the years since, many more quilters have begun using the web to organize their efforts during crises. On the first day of Hurricane Katrina, Jill launched a Quilts for Katrina website. But so many others did the same, she says, "I just looked around and saw who was the most organized and realized it wasn't me. So I shut it down really quickly and joined another organization." And then she made a quilt. ✳

> **Every gun that is made, every warship launched, every rocket fired, signifies, in the final sense, a theft from those who hunger and are not fed, those who are cold and are not clothed.**
>
> DWIGHT D. EISENHOWER

And Still Counting

In early 2007, Caron Lage, a quilter in St. Cloud, Minnesota, saw a photo of a war memorial at Reed College in Oregon. Students had covered the lawn with small red and white flags—3,000 red flags for the American soldiers killed in Iraq and 12,000 white ones, each representing six Iraqi casualties. "I was just overcome with the thought, How come I don't know this?" Caron says. "I check in with the newspaper frequently, and I listen to public radio every day, and I don't know that this many people have died. You hear about a few deaths here and there, but you don't hear totals. And even if you hear big numbers, they're so abstract. Seeing it made it more real."

The Reed memorial was temporary; the flags would be pulled out the next time the grass was mowed. The idea for a more lasting memorial, one that would create the same shocking visual effect, appeared in Caron's head: She would make a quilt to represent both the American and Iraqi casualties and display it wherever she could, both to honor the dead and to provoke people to think about the cost of the war.

Each block in this quilt would represent a U.S. soldier who had died, and black French knots applied to it would represent Iraqis who had lost their lives. Knowing she was going to need a lot of help to reach her initial goal of 3,100 blocks, Caron came up with a design simple enough for anyone with minimal sewing skills to finish and that required only easy-to-find materials: solid-color fabric in any color, batting, and black thread. She divided the estimated Iraqi casualties by the number of American deaths to determine the number of knots per block: 212, which happened to be the boiling point of water in degrees Farenheit. To keep the project simple, she has kept the number of knots constant since then, even though the ratio of civilian to American military deaths has varied over time.

Caron started small and let the project grow organically. She made a few sample blocks, took them to her quilting group, Minnesota Contemporary Quilters, and asked the other members to help. After she put a tutorial on her blog, Caron started to receive blocks from volunteers all over the United States and Canada, and they came in faster and faster as the months progressed. Caron even got her parents involved, and they have since made hundreds of blocks—her mom sews and her dad does the knots.

Caron asks volunteers not to incorporate symbols like peace signs into the blocks because she wants the quilt to remain a memorial, not a protest piece. "I think that it speaks volumes about peace without yelling it in your face," she says. "Sometimes we get so polarized. I didn't want it to exclude anyone who may have lost family members. I didn't want it to feel like it was a protest against their family member choosing to go and fight for us."

At times, being constantly aware of so much death becomes overwhelming. "I've had some dark days," Caron says. But she has grown used to the hundreds of blocks piled behind her furniture in hand-sewn bags. As the quilt has grown, Caron has displayed it several times, including at her church, at an Earth Day celebration, and at a peace picnic held during the Republican National Convention in August 2008. At last count, Caron has accumulated over 1,700 blocks. When she reaches her initial goal of 3,100, she plans to continue making blocks until all the American service members killed in the conflict have been accounted for; she may also begin honoring independent contractors, who haven't been included in either the military or civilian figures she has been using to date.

Each bright block is bound like a miniature quilt, and when displayed, they're safety-pinned together, rather than sewn, to keep the whole quilt flexible and portable. The result is much less somber than most war memorials. "It's really quite pretty," Caron says. And because it's pleasant to look at, she hopes more people—unaccustomed to truly comprehending the full cost of the war—will look unflinchingly at it and acknowledge the lives its blocks and patterns count. ✳

HOW YOU CAN HELP

Make a quilt block or several
(or ask Caron to send you a few blank
blocks), and make 212 French knots on
each block, following the instructions
on page 56. Email Caron at
andstillcounting@yahoo.com to get her
mailing address and send
the blocks to her.

For more information, visit
www.andstillcounting.blogspot.com.

And-Still-Counting Quilt Block

ADAPTED FROM THE AND-STILL-COUNTING PATTERN

Making a quilt block to donate to And Still Counting is a kind of meditation. Each French knot requires care and concentration, which is fitting because it is meant to represent a human life (the block honors an American service member's life lost in Iraq; the 212 French knots honor Iraqi civilian casualties). Choose a pretty, bright color for the background so that your quilt block, when it's displayed along with a few thousand others, will look like a celebration of life as well as a record of loss.

FINISHED SIZE
6 inches square

WHAT YOU'LL NEED
¼ yard of solid-color, 44-inch-wide quilting cotton
(fabric left over will make a second block)

6-inch square of cotton batting

Ruler

Pencil

Black cotton thread

Black pearl cotton

Hand-sewing needle

Embroidery needle

1. From the quilting cotton, cut two 6-inch squares, two 6-inch x 3½-inch rectangles, and two 7½-inch x 3½-inch rectangles.

2. To make a quilt sandwich, lay one of the two 6-inch fabric squares right side down, place the batting square on top of the fabric square, and align the second 6-inch fabric square, right side up, on top.

3. Fold and press each of the 6-inch x 3½-inch rectangles in half length-wise, with wrong sides together. These strips will form the binding for two edges of the 6-inch quilt-block sandwich.

4. Align the long raw edges of one 6-inch binding strip with one edge of the 6-inch quilt sandwich. Machine-stitch the binding strip ½ inch from the sandwich's raw edges. Press the binding away from the top of the sandwich; then fold the binding to the back of the sandwich, turn the sandwich to the wrong side, and pin the binding in place. With the sandwich wrong side up, topstitch the binding in place ¼ inch from the edge. If necessary, trim the edges of the binding to match the edges of the sandwich. Repeat the process with the other 6-inch strip on the sandwich's opposite edge.

5. With the quilt block right side up, repeat Step 4, this time centering each of the two 7½-inch binding strips on the sandwich's remaining raw edges and stitch the strips in place ½ inch from the sandwich's raw edges. Again press the binding strips away from the top of the square. Fold the excess at the ends of the binding toward the back of the quilt, over the edge of the first binding strip, and fold and pin the length of each remaining binding strip.

   Stitch the bindings in place ¼ inch from the edge, leaving extra-long thread tails. Since it's too bulky to backstitch at the end of your topstitching to secure it, pull the top thread's tail to the back of the square and tie it off with the bobbin thread's tail. To finish, thread both tails into a hand needle and stitch into and out of the binding to bury the tails. Then clip the tails close to the fabric.

6. With the quilt block right side up, pencil a dot at its center point. Using this dot as a starting point and your ruler as a guide, mark a horizontal row of 15 dots at ¼-inch intervals—7 on each side of the first dot. Move your ruler up ¼ inch and mark another row of 15 dots. Continue adding rows above and below the first one, until you have 14 rows and 210 dots. Then add 2 more dots as if beginning a 15th row to make 212 marked dots in all.

7. Thread an embroidery needle with pearl cotton and knot the two ends together. To sew a French knot at the first marked dot, bring up the needle from the back to the front of the fabric. Holding the needle on a slant, twist the doubled thread around the needle twice. Holding the wrapped thread tightly against the base of the needle, insert the needle's point back into the fabric very close to, but not actually in, the point where it emerged. Pull the thread through the fabric firmly and evenly to anchor the French knot. Keep the same tension on the thread while twisting it around the needle and pushing the needle back through to the fabric's reverse side. Be sure to pull both strands of thread evenly from the back of the fabric to create a firm, even knot.

   Stitch up through the next marked dot and repeat the process to create the next knot, taking care to line up the knots. Repeat the process until you've made French knots at all the marked points. Tie off the pearl cotton on the back of the quilt block.

Operation
Kid Comfort

In early spring, 2003, Ann Flaherty's son, a Marine, and her son-in-law, an Army Apache pilot, were both deployed to Iraq, where the war was just beginning; the two men reached Baghdad on the same day. At the same time, her stepdaughter was serving in the demilitarized zone at the border of North and South Korea. The situation was stressful for the whole family, but it was especially difficult for Ann's eighteen-month-old grandson, Christian, who couldn't understand why his dad (the Apache pilot) wasn't coming home from work each night. He wouldn't eat or sleep, threw tantrums, and took photos of his dad from the living room and hid them under his crib.

Ann, a quilt artist who had used photo-transfer techniques in her work for years, decided to make Christian a "daddy blanket." She printed photos she'd taken of the boy with his dad onto squares of fabric and sewed them into a quilt. The "touchable, huggable, washable set of photographs" worked—Christian calmed down and started eating and smiling again. He took the quilt everywhere and wouldn't let anybody touch it. After that, Ann made a photo quilt for a boy in Christian's day care whose mother was serving in Afghanistan and whose father was in Iraq. Before long, Ann received a phone call about another child who needed a quilt, and then another, at which point she knew what she was doing was important—and she knew she needed help.

Ann approached several agencies at Fort Bragg Army Base, twelve miles from her home in North Carolina, to find out if they might be interested in a partnership. The director of the Armed Services YMCA was "overjoyed at the idea"; together, they formed Operation Kid Comfort to provide photo-transfer quilts to children from Fort Bragg whose parents were deployed overseas.

The program launched in October 2003. A group of volunteers—mostly women whose husbands were deployed—began meeting regularly at the YMCA to scan photographs, print them onto pretreated fabric, and cut and piece the quilts. No experience was necessary; there were always people on hand to teach newcomers how to use the photo-editing software or the sewing machines. Often, women came to make quilts for their own kids and stayed on as volunteers.

Before long, Ann says, the workshops became "quite a community resource, a lot like an old-fashioned quilting bee. You had the older, seasoned spouses counseling the younger ones over the quilts." The program also brought comfort to the soldiers overseas. "We heard from many of them that their biggest fear was not that they were going to get killed, but that their children were going to forget who they were. They were so grateful that their children were sleeping with those quilts, that their faces were there all the time."

The quilts are astonishingly effective. The little boy who received the second quilt Ann made was inconsolable after his parents were both called up at once. "Before he received his quilt, you couldn't say the word *mom* or *mommy* without him leaving the room," Ann says. "After he received his quilt, his grandmother was standing outside his bedroom listening one evening. He said his prayers with his blankie laid out in front of him, and then he sat down and started telling his parents' pictures about his day."

Operation Kid Comfort groups have now been established at Armed Services YMCAs from Fort Drumm in New York to Naval Base San Diego in California, as well as in Alaska, Hawaii, and Germany. Civilian quilting guilds, church groups, and individuals also help out by donating supplies and assembling quilts. At Fort Bragg alone, more than 3,000 families have received quilts. Operation Kid Comfort asks the families that receive quilts to follow just one rule: The quilts must be used. "They're not keepsakes, they're not to hang on the wall," Ann says. "They're made to withstand everything a kid will do to them."

Ann's grandson, Christian, kept close track of his quilt even after his dad returned from Iraq. When he was about three or four, Ann asked him if she could borrow it; she wanted to show it to someone who was interested in volunteering for Operation Kid Comfort. "He said, 'Well, when are you going to have it back? Who's going to touch it? Nobody's going to touch it, are they?' It was that precious to him. I had to assure him it would be back in his hands in two hours." Ann's son-in-law, Mike, was deployed to Iraq again in 2005, when Christian's little brother, Joshua, was eighteen months old, the same age Christian had been when Mike left the first time. Ann made sure Joshua's quilt was ready before his dad left. Now, with Mike home again safe and sound, both quilts remain precious possessions. ✳

HOW YOU CAN HELP

If you live near Fort Bragg in North Carolina, Fort Drumm in New York, Fort Riley in Kansas, or Camp Pendleton in San Diego, and you'd like to help out at Operation Kid Comfort meetings, contact the Armed Services YMCA on the base. For more information on these meetings, or for guidelines on volunteering, visit the Operation Kid Comfort link at www.asymca.org.

No matter where you live, you can volunteer to quilt and finish Operation Kid Comfort quilts at home. Call the Armed Services YMCA's national office at 800-597-1260 for more information.

CHAPTER THREE

Quilting for Kids

The world can be an especially frightening place for its youngest inhabitants. But simple things can have an almost magical effect on anxious children, and quilts seem to hold extra-special comforting powers. Linda Arye, founder of Quilts for Kids (see page 66), explains it this way: "Somehow, when you get under the covers, the whole world goes away, and it's just you in a safe haven. And I guess that's what the quilts do. They provide a safe haven for these kids."

The powerful effect of quilting for kids in need is not a new discovery. In 1914, a visitor to St. Joseph's Orphanage in Winnipeg, Canada, described a room in which dozens of boys slept: "A peep into the large dormitory, on the third floor, shows a kaleidoscopic vista of bright patchwork quilts, covering little white iron beds, that dwindle away down the ward in six long orderly rows." The quilts were symbols of home and warmth; their patterns distinguished one boy's bed from another's.

Nearly a century later, handmade patchwork quilts stitched by faraway quilters brighten rows of beds in orphanages in China, Russia, India, Haiti, Mexico, and many other countries. In the United States, there are huge numbers of kids in need: More than 13 million children live below the federal poverty level, more than 1.3 million are homeless at some point in any given year, and more than half a million are in foster care. And no matter what a family's circumstances, kids can't always be protected from harm; little ones fall ill and have accidents every day.

Whatever a child's predicament, handmade patchwork quilts make particularly good security blankets because each one is special. Any parent who has tried to replace a child's lost blanket knows its uniqueness matters, but research has actually proved this to be the case. In a 2007 study conducted by Professor Bruce Hood from the University of Bristol and Dr. Paul Bloom from Yale University, researchers showed children between the ages of three and six a scientific-looking machine and told them it could copy any object. (It was actually a cabinet filled with replicas of the children's toys used in the experiment.) Other toys were okay to copy, but when the researchers tried to copy the special toy or blanket each of them slept with at night, a quarter of the children refused to let the object be copied at all, and most of the others demanded the original back.

All the projects in this chapter are small, but no less special for their size—especially considering how much they will mean to their recipients.

Binky Patrol

Susan Finch believes that every child who's scared or hurting needs a "binky"—a security blanket. And thanks to Binky Patrol, tens of thousands of quilts and blankets have been given to children who need comfort.

Susan started Binky Patrol when she was going through a difficult time herself. In 1996, she was working sixty hours a week at an art gallery in Pasadena, California, and her marriage was failing. To distract herself from her problems and find a little peace one night a week, she learned to quilt and started a quilting circle with a few friends. Around the same time, she organized a successful fund-raiser at her art gallery for a local battered women's shelter. Susan found much comfort both in quilting and in helping others, and her mother suggested the obvious—that she combine the two and make quilts for children at the shelter.

Susan is the kind of person who flies into action when she gets excited. She came up with a plan not only to make quilts for the local shelter, but also to organize quilters to make blankets for children with HIV/AIDS and other serious health problems. She decided on a name for her new organization, Binky Patrol, convinced local clothing manufacturers to donate fabric, and asked picture framers who did work for the gallery to give her scraps of silk and cotton left over from the framing process. She sent out a press release about Binky Patrol and put a volunteer sign-up sheet outside her gallery.

Binky Patrol's volunteers hadn't even held their first meeting when something astonishing happened. Susan received a call from one of Oprah Winfrey's producers, who had seen the press release and wanted to include Binky Patrol in an upcoming show on children with AIDS. A fifteen-second mention on Oprah's show turned Susan's life upside down. Hundreds of people called from all over the country, wanting to make quilts and start chapters. She didn't even have voicemail on her phone, a problem she quickly rectified by flagging down two men from the phone company who happened to be walking by and convincing them to install it on the spot. In less than three months, Binky Patrol became a national nonprofit organization; in the years since, it's grown to eighty-five chapters and at least 20,000 volunteers.

Today, Binky Patrol distributes blankets to kids who need them with the help of a huge variety of agencies and volunteer groups. Among them are Babies out of Bondage, an organization that cares for the children of inmates in a women's prisons in California's Central Valley; Hope Haven, a clinic for kids with developmental disabilities in Jacksonville, Florida; a county sheriff's department in central Texas; grief-counseling groups at schools in upstate New York; Bikers Against Child Abuse in Oklahoma; and a summer camp for young burn victims in Washington State.

More than a decade after starting Binky Patrol, Susan is happily remarried, with two young children and a full-time job in public relations. She's even busier than before, but she manages to keep Binky Patrol going because of her insistence on keeping things as low-key and decentralized as possible. Binky Patrol's guidelines are simple. "It shouldn't be hard to volunteer," Susan says. Volunteers make quilts in any patterns they please, and the organization accepts knitted and crocheted blankets as well. Binkies have to be soft, and they have to be tough enough to endure frequent washing and drying.

"Think about what the goal is," Susan says about making binkies. "If the goal is to comfort a child, take all the other stuff out of it. Take out the 'I want it to line up, I want it to match this picture.' Bring it down to the simplest goal you have: What would comfort a child?" ✳

HOW YOU CAN HELP

Binky Patrol donates quilts to babies, children, and teens. Think about the child's age when you make a quilt. If it's for a toddler, don't make it too heavy to be kicked off at night. If it's for an older child, the colors shouldn't be babyish. Binky Patrol is always short on quilts for boys between ages twelve and eighteen.

When choosing fabric and stitching, remember that binkies must be able to withstand frequent machine-washing in hot water and machine-drying.

Binkies should be at least 36 inches square, unless they are intended for preemies or to tuck babies into car seats and strollers.

Donate completed binkies to a local chapter (go to **www.binkypatrol.org** for a list of chapters and calendar of events). If there isn't a chapter near you, mail binkies to the closest chapter or to the organization's headquarters in Oregon:
Binky Patrol, Inc.
PO Box 652
Beaverton, OR 97075-0652

Easy, Striped Baby Quilt

ADAPTED FROM A PATTERN BY BINKY PATROL FOUNDER SUSAN FINCH

A good security blanket should be unique. The fabric should be interesting and, at the same time, soothing. To get started, choose a couple of bright, complex prints, then add a solid and a calmer print for balance. You can easily adapt this pattern to different sizes by changing the length and width of the strips.

FINISHED SIZE

Approximately 36 inches x 49 inches

WHAT YOU'LL NEED

½ yard each of four 44-inch-wide flannel or soft cotton fabrics (for quilt top)

1½ yards of 44-inch-wide flannel or soft cotton fabric (for backing)

¼ yard of contrasting cotton fabric (for traditional binding—if you choose a mock binding, you won't need this)

Crib-size (46 inches x 60 inches), lightweight cotton batting

Matching cotton thread

SEWING INSTRUCTIONS

1. From each of the ½-yard pieces of fabric, cut one 3-inch x 36-inch strip, one 4½-inch x 36-inch strip, and one 5½-inch x 36-inch strip.

2. Lining up their long sides, arrange the 12 strips into an order you like. Then, with right sides together, sew the long edge of each successive neighboring pair of strips with a ¼-inch seam, and press the seam allowances together to the side with the darker fabric.

3. Make a quilt sandwich of the three layers, and pin-baste the layers together (see page 128).

4. Machine-quilt the quilt sandwich (see page 128). A simple grid pattern works well for this quilt. Keep the lines no more than 5 inches apart.

5. Bind the quilt with either a traditional binding or a mock binding (see pages 129–130).

Quilts for Kids

In August 2000, interior designer Linda Arye was placing a fabric order for a client at the Philadelphia Design Center when she spotted a mountain of industrial-size garbage bags at the back of a showroom. They were full of leftover samples of discontinued designer fabrics, some of which cost more than a hundred dollars a yard. "It'll be in the Philadelphia landfill by tomorrow," the manager told her. Horrified by the waste, Linda told him not to get rid of the fabric—she'd figure out what to do with it. By the time she arrived home, she had a plan. She would turn those squares of fabric into quilts for seriously ill children in local hospitals. When Linda's own daughter, Molly, was small, she had been hospitalized with a life-threatening illness. Molly survived, but Linda never forgot how frightening the experience had been for her daughter, and she knew how much comfort something as simple as a quilt would have brought her.

Linda had never quilted in her life; in fact, she'd flunked sixth-grade home ec. She called the only two people she knew who could sew—her Aunt Barbara and a neighbor, also named Barbara—and told them about her idea for Quilts for Kids. Both women agreed to make quilts and to help her find others willing to participate.

Linda talked the managers of other showrooms in the Philadelphia Design Center into saving fabric for her, and when she spoke to her contacts at major fabric companies, she found out they threw out enormous amounts of fabric, too. Bolts of discontinued fabric took up valuable warehouse space for months before being discarded, so the fabric companies were happy to deliver all that extra fabric to Linda's house. Luckily, she and her husband had just finished building an addition; their new sunroom became Quilts for Kids' office, workroom, and storeroom.

During Quilts for Kids' first year, Linda kept the organization's efforts local. She convinced editors at newspapers in nearby towns to run stories about Quilts for Kids, which helped her recruit volunteers. She continued her design work, but she asked her clients to make their checks out to Quilts for Kids. That year, which Linda refers to as the organization's "toddler" phase, volunteers made about 500 quilts for patients at the Children's Hospital of Philadelphia and other nearby hospitals, as well as children in local shelters.

Quilts for Kids grew up fast the following year—2001—in the aftermath of the September 11 attacks. Yardley, Pennsylvania, where Linda lives, is about an hour and a half commute from Manhattan, and eleven of the town's residents were killed. The pilot of the second plane to hit the World Trade Center lived just up the street from Linda. The town supervisor's son died in one of the towers.

Ellen Kravet, head of Kravet Fabric, a large fabric company based in New York, and a member of Quilts for Kids' fledgling board, called Linda and offered to donate some red, white, and blue fabric to be made into quilts for children who had lost family members in the Twin Towers. When Ellen said *some*, she meant four eighteen-wheelers' worth. Within a couple of days, almost 40,000 pounds of fabric from New York fabric companies arrived at Linda's house—much more than enough to make the roughly 5,000 quilts that would be needed. It was so much fabric, in fact, that Linda had to go door to door on her street, asking neighbors if she could borrow space in their garages. She mobilized her volunteers immediately and began fund-raising to cover the cost of shipping the quilts. That was the beginning of Quilts for Kids' Red, White, and Blue Project.

Neighbors, including those who had lost loved ones in the attack, gathered at Linda's house to cut and fold red, white, and blue fabric to send to volunteer quilters all over the country. The house was full of activity, with people coming and going, carrying boxes in and out, but it was almost completely silent. When the news crawl on *Dateline NBC* included Quilts for Kids in a list of organizations working to help the victims' families, Linda began receiving hundreds of phone calls and thousands of e-mails a day from people who wanted to participate and others suggesting families who needed quilts. A woman called from California to ask that a quilt be donated to a family in Pennsylvania. Linda took down the address; the street was just one over from her own.

Since the Red, White, and Blue Project, Quilts for Kids has grown into a huge organization with chapters in thirty-one states and tens of thousands of volunteers who sew about 10,000 quilts a year. Soon after September 11, Linda quit her job. "I could not put my heart and soul into interior design work any longer," she says. "I had a new love, and it was this charity, which still needed me to guide it and nurture it." In addition to Linda, three women now work part-time at national headquarters, which is still in Linda's house. They put together quilt kits—donated fabric, instructions, and a Quilts for Kids label to be sewn onto the finished quilt—and send them out to stitchers across the country. The kits aren't required—Quilts for Kids accepts quilts made from quilters'

> "
>
> **How wonderful it is that nobody need wait a single moment before starting to improve the world.**
>
> "
>
> ANNE FRANK

own fabric stashes, too, as well as other handmade gifts for sick kids, like fabric-covered diaries and many-pocketed bags to hang over hospital bed rails. Every weekday, Mike, the UPS driver, whose son received a quilt when he was hospitalized in Philadelphia, delivers packages of completed quilts. The staff never tires of opening up the boxes and admiring their contents. Often, all the quilts in a box have been pieced using the same patchwork design—many of the quilt kits include pinwheel patterns, for example—but their colors vary wildly, and each is quilted in its maker's own style.

A concern for the environment and reducing waste has motivated Quilts for Kids since the beginning. In 2002, Linda linked design centers and fabric wholesalers all over the country with nearby communities of quilters interested in community service, focusing on the local benefits of recycling all that fabric. "I'd say to them, by putting renewable resources in landfills, you're leaving a legacy for your children and grandchildren. And people would say, 'Not in my backyard, not in my landfill.'"

Quilts for Kids encourages its volunteers to start locally, but not to stop there. Anywhere the group sees a need, it finds a way to meet it. Within a couple of days of Hurricane Katrina, for example, Quilts for Kids volunteers in the Houston area delivered thousands of quilts to the Astrodome. Quilts for Kids sends quilts to AIDS orphanages in Johannesburg, South Africa, and to Hillel Yaffe Medical Center in Hadera, Israel. When fabric companies donate heavyweight fabric like velvet and brocade, the Quilts for Kids staff gives it to Lutheran World Relief, an organization working to alleviate global poverty. LWF's volunteers use the fabric to make warm winter quilts for kids in Russia and Romania who've been released from orphanages at age twelve or thirteen and must now sleep on the streets.

> "
>
> It is comforting when one has a sorrow to lie in the warmth of one's bed and there, abandoning all effort and all resistance, to bury even one's head under the cover...
>
> "
>
> MARCEL PROUST
> from *Regrets, Reveries, Changing Skies,*
> no. 11, "Pleasures and Regrets"

According to the American Academy of Pediatrics, young adults may be cared for by pediatricians until the age of twenty-one, or in special circumstances, later. Quilts for Kids uses the same rule. That means that many of the wounded servicemen and women returning from Iraq and Afghanistan still qualify for quilts. The Annapolis chapter of Quilts for Kids makes regular deliveries to wounded soldiers at Walter Reed Medical Center in Washington, D.C.—and they sneak plenty of quilts in for older patients, too. There's a Quilts for Kids chapter at Fort Dix in New Jersey, as well, where soldiers—including senior officers—make quilts for local hospitals while they wait to be deployed. Most of the Fort Dix volunteers are men, and, Linda says, quilting comes to them quite naturally. On at least one occasion, the soldier who started a quilt hasn't made it back from Iraq, and a fellow Fort Dix quilter has finished it.

The quilts often have a magically calming effect on the kids who receive them. Once, when Linda was delivering quilts to a children's oncology unit at a New Jersey hospital, she heard terrible screaming coming from one of the rooms. A small, pink-nightgowned girl was wailing and rubbing at her incision while her father tried in vain to stop her. Every single thing in the room was pink, so Linda grabbed the pinkest quilt out of the pile she'd brought. She knew that if she tried to talk to the screaming child, she'd only yell louder, but if she whispered, the girl would stop and try to hear her. She leaned close to the girl and whispered that she'd brought her a gift. "All I did was put a quilt on her," Linda says, but it worked. The girl quieted. She even managed to smile. And then she fell asleep. ✹

HOW YOU CAN HELP

Contact your local Quilts for Kids chapter to find out the specific needs of your community. You can find a list of chapters at www.quiltsforkids.org. If there isn't a chapter near you, call Quilts for Kids headquarters at 215-295-5484.

You can request a quilt kit, which provides enough fabric to finish a quilt, plus a pattern and instructions, or you can make a quilt from scratch, using any pattern you'd like for a kid of any age. The pattern on page 70 is one Quilts for Kids suggests for premature babies.

Quilts should be lightweight, made with low-loft batting, and machine-quilted rather then tied since quilts used in hospitals have to be sturdy enough to stand up to washing in heavy-duty industrial washing machines.

Many domestic cotton mills have closed in recent years, and, as a result, manufacturers can't donate as much fabric to Quilts for Kids as they could in the past. If you have unused kid-friendly cotton you'd like to donate, contact the staff at the phone number above or e-mail Linda at linda.arye@quiltsforkids.org.

Preemie Pinwheel Quilt

ADAPTED FROM A QUILTS FOR KIDS PATTERN

This quilt is intended for the tiniest inhabitants of hospitals—prematurely born babies. It is big enough to cover an isolette in a neonatal intensive care unit in order to block light and sound while the baby sleeps. It's also small enough not to overwhelm a tiny preemie when he or she goes home.

FINISHED SIZE

34 inches square

WHAT YOU'LL NEED

¼ yard each of four 44-inch-wide, soft cotton fabrics in at least 2 contrasting colors (solid color or solid with dots and stripes works well) (for pinwheels)

½ yard of 44-inch-wide white muslin (for sashing)

½ yard of contrasting cotton fabric (for cornerstones and binding)

1¼ yards of 44-inch-wide soft cotton (for backing)

Craft-sized (46 inches x 36 inches) thin cotton batting

Matching cotton thread

Quilter's ruler

SEWING INSTRUCTIONS

1. Cut sixteen 4¼-inch squares from each of the four pinwheel fabrics.

2. Cut twenty-four 6-inch x 2-inch strips from the muslin for the sashing.

3. Cut four 2-inch-deep, selvedge-to-selvedge strips from the muslin for the borders.

4. Cut nine 2-inch squares from the cornerstone fabric.

5. For each pinwheel, choose four squares, two of one color and two of another. Align two different-colored squares with right sides together. Using quilter's chalk and a ruler, mark a diagonal line on the wrong side of one of the aligned squares from one corner to the opposite corner. Sew two diagonal seams parallel to the chalked line, ¼ inch away from it on each side (see Diagram A on page 73). Using your rotary cutter and cutting mat, cut along the chalked line. Open up each half-square triangle unit, and press the seam allowances together toward the darker fabric.

   Repeat the process above with the other two squares. Then trim each half-square triangle unit to 3½ inches square.

6. Arrange the four half-square triangle units into a pinwheel pattern (see Diagram B). Then, with right sides together and their edges aligned, sew the top two units together along one side with a ¼-inch seam, and press the seam allowances toward the darker fabric. (Note that, for all the remaining seams mentioned in the directions below, you'll likewise position the pieces right sides together with their edges aligned, and join them with a ¼-inch seam.)

Repeat the process above with the bottom two half-square triangle units. Finally sew the top and bottom rows together to complete the pinwheel, with rights sides together and the edges aligned; and press the seam allowances to one side (either side is okay).

Repeat this step to create 15 more pinwheels.

7. Sew the pinwheel blocks into four rows of four blocks (see Diagram C), with sashing between each block, and press the seam allowances toward the blocks.

8. To make a long sashing strip to go between each pair of rows, sew four 6-inch x 2-inch sashing strips into one long strip, placing cornerstones between each pair of strips (see Diagram D).

Repeat this step twice more.

9. Sew the four rows of pinwheel blocks together with long sashing strips between each pair of rows, taking care to match the edges of the cornerstones with the edges of the vertical sashing pieces.

10. Sew a long border strip to the top, and then sew another border strip to the bottom of the quilt top. Trim both ends of each strip even with the edge of the quilt top. Repeat the process to sew long border strips to the quilt's other two sides, and again trim the ends even with the edge of the quilt.

11. Layer the quilt top, batting, and backing into a quilt sandwich, and pin-baste the three layers (see page 128).

12. Beginning from the center and moving outward, machine-quilt two curved lines that meet at both ends inside each blade of each pinwheel; then quilt meandering lines (see page 130) around the pinwheels. Alternatively, outline-quilt (see page 131) within each triangle and each cornerstone.

13. Bind the quilt with a traditional binding, following the directions on page 129.

Newborns in Need

A mother of six, grandmother of five, and the youngest of fourteen children, Carol Green knows babies. She can lay her arm down next to an infant, make a mark on her skin near her elbow, and gather enough information to sew a little outfit that fits perfectly without resorting once to a pattern. Carol has been sewing and quilting (and smocking, crocheting, tatting—you name it) since she was a little girl. These skills have all been instrumental in her current calling—as organizer of Newborns in Need—a charity geared toward making much-needed items for the smallest recipients.

In 1992, Carol read an article in a magazine about a woman who sewed tiny burial gowns and gave them to her local hospital for babies who died at birth. No one is ever prepared for such an event; many families are too distraught to solve the problem of what to bury their baby in, and others simply can't afford to buy something special. "Babies were being buried in paper sacks," Carol says. "I just about came unglued." At the time, her youngest daughter was a year old. Carol had made many baby quilts for that one child, and she couldn't stop thinking about all those babies who didn't have a thing.

She called a hospital near her home in Kansas City, Missouri, and asked if they needed any help. A nurse invited her in for a meeting, and when Carol got there, she couldn't believe how sterile the neonatal intensive care unit looked. When she asked why there were no bumper pads, colorful blankets, or quilts, the nurse told her that each incubator cost nearly $60,000; there wasn't room in the budget for pretty bedding. Carol drove directly from the hospital to a fabric store in a nearby shopping plaza, where she convinced the owner to donate bolts of flannel. She enlisted some of her friends, and they sewed and sewed and sewed. They made bumper pads, receiving blankets, little hats, and gowns, and by the next month, the Kansas City NICU looked like a proper nursery. The seeds of Newborns in Need were sown.

A few months later, Carol and her family moved to Houston, a small town in the middle of the Missouri Ozarks, about two and a half hours southwest of St. Louis. "It's a beautiful, beautiful place to live," Carol says, "very lush and very green, but there's no employment." In Texas County, twice as many children live in poverty as the national average. Carol has visited log cabins up in the hills with dirt floors, blankets pinned up instead of front doors, and quilts thrown on the floor in place of beds. When she saw the overwhelming needs of her new community, Carol got to work.

For the next six years, Carol and a committed group of volunteers provided quilts and blankets, baby clothes, and tiny burial garments to families, agencies, and hospitals in Missouri and neighboring states. After a full day of home-schooling her children and taking care of the house and garden, Carol would start sewing, often staying up well past midnight to finish a project. In the winter, she always kept extra baby clothes and quilts in her truck. When she saw a young mother in a store with an underdressed baby and hardly anything in her cart, she'd whisper to her kids to run out to the car. She'd engage the mother in conversation and compliment the baby, and by the time she was done, the mother's shopping cart would be full of warm things and the baby all bundled up.

"I really believe in OTM," Carol says. "OTM is 'Open Thy Mouth,' and I do that real well. I never shut up. Everywhere I went—churches, gas stations, realtors—if somebody said to me, 'How's your day going?' I'd tell them. I started sharing with people what the need was, and Newborns in Need just grew."

In 1998, a government grant gave Carol the resources she needed to transform Newborns in Need from a local effort into a national organization. She set up an office, hired a small volunteer staff and a part-time bookkeeper, and applied for nonprofit status. Within eighteen months, thirty-four chapters were established; a decade later, there are forty-seven chapters in thirty states. Eleven thousand volunteers now send out 35,000 baby necessities a month, including store-bought items like bottles, diapers, and strollers, as well as handmade quilts, clothes, toys, and burial outfits.

As is so often true, Newborns in Need volunteers get as much out of their work as the recipients do. "I wish I had a nickel," Carol says, "for every older lady who has said to me, 'My children are grown, my husband is gone, I'm here with my cats, I'm useless.' And the first thing out of my mouth is, 'Absolutely not. I need you so badly.' I talk to them even a month later, and they say, 'I'm so grateful for Newborns in Need.'"

Although she modeled some aspects of her organization on her own church, the Church of Jesus Christ of Latter Day Saints, Newborns in Need is nondenominational. "We don't discriminate whatsoever," Carol says. "Baptists and Catholics and Mormons and holy-rollers, atheists, even Wiccans, we all just work shoulder to shoulder…Babies transcend all barriers." ✳

HOW YOU CAN HELP

Newborns in Need can find a home for almost any baby items, from handmade quilts and receiving blankets to store-bought necessities like diapers and bottles.

Make the Bib and Burp Cloth on page 76, or contact your local chapter or the Newborns in Need national office and ask for other fast, easy sewing projects for preemies and other hospitalized infants.

Donated quilts, blankets, and baby clothes must be machine-washable and -dryable.

Go to www.newbornsinneed.org for a list of chapters, or contact nationaloffice@newbornsinneed.org for other shipping locations.

Bib and Matching Burp Cloth

ADAPTED FROM A NEWBORNS IN NEED PATTERN

Sometimes the basics are what's needed most. In a couple of hours you can whip up a baby bib and matching burp cloth. Try experimenting with nontraditional fabrics for babies—this pattern works well in fun, surprising prints. If you're feeling adventurous, try making your own bias tape for the ties. It isn't difficult; you just need a bias-tape maker and some cute, soft fabric that will feel good on babies' necks.

FINISHED SIZE

Bib: 7½" wide x 8" long; **Burp Cloth:** 9½" wide x 17" long

WHAT YOU'LL NEED

Two scraps of different quilting cottons, one about 4 inches x 2 inches and another 8 inches x 15 inches (for pieced blocks)

¼ yard of another 44-inch-wide quilting cotton (for background)

¼ yard of 44-inch-wide cotton terry cloth

28 inches of ⅜-inch-wide double-fold bias tape (linen tape is preferable since polyester/cotton bias tape is very harsh on babies' skin)

Bib template on page 78 (photocopy template at 200 percent; fold paper that's twice template's width in half vertically, position template's straight edge on paper's fold, and cut around the curved edges; then unfold the paper pattern)

Juice glass about 3 inches in diameter

SEWING INSTRUCTIONS

For blocks

1. From one of the two scrap fabrics, cut four "not-quite-squares" that are about 1½ inches to 1¾ inches on each side. Use a ruler to keep each side straight, but don't worry about exact measurements or right angles (a little variance gives the block some character).

2. From the other scrap fabric, cut four strips about 1½ inches wide x 15 inches long—again, the measurements don't have to be exact. With right sides together, align the edge of one strip with one edge of a not-quite-square, and sew the two edges together with a ¼-inch seam (note that for all the steps below, you'll also use a ¼-inch seam).

3. Trim the excess strip at the end of the seam, and press the seam allowances toward the darker fabric. Turn the block 90 degrees, and sew the rest of the strip that you just cut off across the end of the first strip to the next side of the not-quite-square. Trim the excess at the end, and press the seam allowances toward the darker fabric. Turn the block again, and repeat the process above twice more (see Diagram A on page 78). Trim the pieced block down to a 3-inch x 3½-inch rectangle.

4. Repeat steps 1-3 until you have four pieced blocks.

For bib

1. To make the front of the bib, cut one 3½-inch x 5½-inch piece and one 3½-inch x 4-inch piece of background fabric. Sew these to the opposite sides of one block to form a 3½-inch-wide x by 11½-inch-long strip (see Diagram B on page 78). Press the seam allowances toward the darker fabric.

2. Cut two 3½-inch x 11½-inch strips of background fabric. Sew these to each side of the strip you just pieced (see Diagram C on page 78). Press the seam allowances toward the darker fabric.

BIB TEMPLATE

Photocopy at 200%

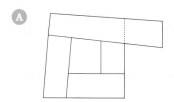

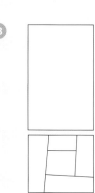

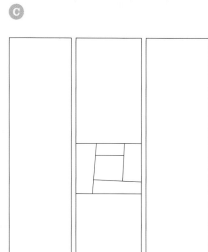

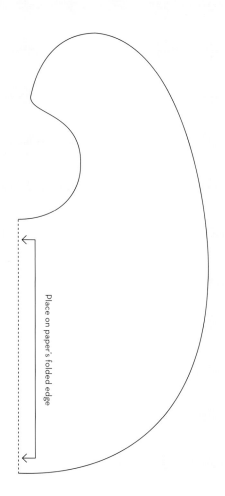

Place on paper's folded edge

3. Pin the bib template to the pieced bib front, centering the block below the neck opening, and cut around the template.

4. Pin the bib template to a piece of terry cloth, and likewise cut around template.

5. Align the bib top and terry-cloth bib together, with right sides facing, and sew the front to the back around the outside edge, leaving the neck open.

6. Turn the bib right side out, and edge-stitch (see page 130) the neckline closed near the raw edges.

7. Topstitch (see page 131) around the rest of the bib ¼ inch from the outside edge.

8. Stitch-in-the-ditch (see page 131) around the block and the uneven square inside it.

9. To make the tie at the bib's neck, start by marking the center point of the 28-inch length of double-fold bias tape with a pin. Fold the width of the bias tape around the bib's neck to encase this edge, matching the center of the tape with the center of the neckline. Pin the bias tape carefully in place around the neck, using lots of pins.

10. Fold in each end of the bias tape at a 45-degree angle (see Diagram D), and pin the folded ends in place. Then, starting at one end of the bias tape, edge-stitch the tape closed, lockstitching or backstitching (see page 130) at the beginning of your stitching to secure it. When you get to the neckline, keep edge-stitching the bias tape, being careful to catch it on the wrong side. Continue edge-stitching all the way to the other end of the bias tape, and again lockstitch or backstitch at the end of your stitching. Press the bib and bias tape flat.

For burp cloth

1. Cut two 3½-inch x 2¾-inch pieces of the background fabric. Sew these rectangles between three of the pieced blocks you made earlier to make a 3½-inch-wide x 13½-inch-long strip. Cut two 3½-inch x 4½-inch pieces of the background fabric, and sew one to each end of the strip with a ¼-inch seam. Press all the seam allowances toward the darker fabric.

2. Cut two 20-inch x 4½-inch strips of background fabric, and sew one strip to each long edge of the strip containing the blocks. Press the seam allowances toward the darker fabric.

3. Trim this fabric panel to 17½ inches x 10 inches. To round the corners, place the juice glass upside down on one corner, and trace around it with a chalk fabric marker. Repeat this on the other corners, and then, using fabric scissors, cut along the curved line.

4. For the burp cloth backing, repeat step 3, substituting terry cloth for the fabric panel.

5. With right sides together, sew the two pieces together, leaving a 2½-inch opening on one edge for turning the work right side out.

6. Turn the burp cloth right side out. Topstitch around the entire piece ¼ inch from the edge. At the opening, fold the seam's raw edges in evenly and continue topstitching to close the opening. Lockstitch or backstitch at the end of your stitching.

7. Stitch-in-the-ditch around each block and each not-quite-square.

Wrap Them in Love

In 1980, Ellen and Scott Sime drove to the Seattle airport to add a six-month-old girl from Korea to their growing family. Five other babies flew in with their new daughter, Kimberly, and their expectant parents waited along with the Simes. The new parents all had cameras with them and lots of baby gear, and some had brought along grandparents and friends. As the babies came through customs, the families watched, trying to guess which of the little ones was theirs. Each baby wore a hospital bracelet on both arms, one bearing the child's name, the other his or her future family's name. "They looked at the name and asked us who we were, and then just handed us a baby," Ellen remembers. "And we went walking out of the airport carrying her. It was just amazing." A couple of years after Kimberly's adoption, they adopted another child from Korea, a boy, who was almost four at the time.

The most difficult part of the adoption process was the waiting. Ellen found it excruciating to have just a picture and a little bit of information, to know her children were thousands of miles away but not to know what was happening to them.

After going through that experience twice, she couldn't help thinking about all the other children waiting in orphanages all over the world. She wanted to find a way to help them, but as the working mother of five children with only three and a half years between the oldest and the youngest, Ellen says—and this must be an understatement—she was pretty busy. Still, she never forgot those orphans.

Ellen has sewn her own clothes since the age of ten, so for her, it had been a natural progression to quilting, and then to owning a fabric store and working as a professional machine quilter. One day, as she was sewing a baby quilt for a store display, it occurred to her that a handmade quilt might comfort a child in an orphanage. Her youngest had turned eighteen that year; there was nothing keeping Ellen from starting a big, new project. But if she was going to make quilts for so many children who needed them, she was going to need help. That's why, in 1998, she started the Wrap Them in Love Foundation.

Ellen launched the organization by holding a "big quilting weekend" at her store. "We started out with just a few volunteers, and by the end of the weekend, there were a few more because people would come in off the street. I invited the newspaper to come in and see what we were doing, so there was something in the newspaper about all these crazy ladies quilting." But she didn't stop there. She created a website and a Yahoo group and began attracting hundreds of volunteers from all over the United States and a handful of other countries. In Oregon and Alabama, for example, local groups formed just to make quilts for Wrap Them in Love. Ellen's account of the Oregon group's beginning is typical of charity quilting efforts: "A woman in Portland was in line in her local quilt store and said she'd really like to find some other people to quilt with and make quilts for charity. The quilt store owner said, 'Well you can meet here once a month.' And the quilter said, 'That's great, but I'm just one person.' And then the person behind her said, 'I'll come and quilt with you.' And so then there were two." That sort of openness and generosity is common among quilters, Ellen says.

Ellen keeps a big map on the wall in her store, with pins marking the locations where Wrap Them in Love has sent quilts. Guatemala, Haiti, India, Thailand, Bulgaria, Kazakhstan, Iraq—she never seems to have enough pins to keep up. The foundation doesn't send quilts overseas by mail. The cost of international shipping is far too high, and Ellen would never know for sure if the quilts reached their destinations. Instead, she relies on travelers to carry quilts in their luggage. Adoptive families picking up children and church groups going to volunteer at orphanages take extra suitcases. Often people going on vacation, visiting family, or going on business trips offer to deliver quilts. When her son went to visit his girlfriend in Japan, he dropped off twenty-one quilts at an orphanage. Ellen has become an expert at packing quilts as efficiently as possible: Each one is rolled up into a tight little sausage and tied with ribbon or string. More than 11,000 quilts donated by quilting guilds, online quilting groups, and individual volunteers have been carried all over the world in this way.

Wrap Them in Love quilts have a way of arriving in what turns out to be precisely the time and place they're most needed. A priest Ellen knows works at an orphanage in Russia. Once, after he'd been on leave in the States, he returned to the orphanage—where 124 children were living—with 125 quilts. That night, a little girl was found in a garbage heap and brought to the orphanage. She was about three, exactly the right size for the one unclaimed quilt. Another time, a woman and her daughter took some quilts to an orphanage in South America. The nuns didn't know they were coming, so it must have been a coincidence that just the night before, they'd been praying for new bedding for the children in time for the winter.

"We could take the money we spend on these quilts and just go buy a bunch of blankets, but it wouldn't be the same at all," Ellen says. "When we make quilts, we put tons and tons of love into them, and I think the kids feel that love." According to the director of an orphanage in Thailand, they feel something else equally important: a sense of ownership

> "
> There can be
> no keener revelation
> of a society's soul
> than the way in which it
> treats its children.
> "
>
> NELSON MANDELA

and pride. The quilts are often the only bright spots in an otherwise dull and dreary environment, and they're also often the only possessions that belong to each child, the only things they don't have to share with anybody else. That's another reason the uniqueness of each quilt matters.

When sending quilts internationally, of course, Ellen finds that cultural issues can crop up. For example, if a quilt is going to a Muslim child, it can't have certain animals on it. And colors have different associations in different cultures. Sometimes that's fortunate. Once Ellen sent a shipment of quilts to a group of teenage boys in a Mexican orphanage. Struggling to come up with enough quilts big enough for nearly grown boys, she ended up including two or three pink quilts, though she was sure the boys wouldn't like them. To her surprise, the most popular of all, the one they argued over, turned out to be the brightest, pinkest one.

"The teenage kids love them as much as the little kids do," Ellen says. "We're grown-ups, and we love to snuggle up in quilts. And so you can imagine if you're a child who has nobody and you're all by yourself, or you've been through some kind of traumatic crisis, how great it is to wrap up in a quilt and feel that love from all those people who've touched it along the way." ✳

HOW YOU CAN HELP

Wrap Them in Love accepts finished quilts, quilt tops, and individual blocks. They prefer that finished quilts measure about 40 inches x 60 inches, but smaller and larger ones are accepted.

Wrap Them in Love suggests that you place ties or quilting lines close together to make the quilt extra durable and that you sew a label onto the quilt that includes your name, the town where you live, and the date you made the quilt.

To volunteer to deliver a bagful of quilts while traveling to a developing country, to find out more about fund-raising efforts, or to send donations, contact:
Ellen Sime
Wrap Them in Love Foundation
2522-A Old Hwy 99 S
Mt. Vernon, WA 98273
www.wraptheminlove.org

Softies for Mirabel

Softies for Mirabel is a holiday toy drive with a twenty-first-century twist. The toy animals and dolls are made the old-fashioned way (each "softie" is handmade and unique), and they're all donated to a single organization (the Mirabel Foundation, in Melbourne, Australia); but the collection effort is digital and international. Pip Lincolne, the organizational force behind Softies for Mirabel, is a crafter and blogger who runs an unusually named shop, Meet Me at Mike's, down the street from the Mirabel Foundation in Melbourne's Fitzroy neighborhood.

Pip sells crafts made by young designers just getting started—everything from quilts, clothes, and aprons to stationery, jewelry, and toys. Named after both Pip's cat and Mike D. from the Beastie Boys, the store reflects Pip's crafty, nostalgic sensibility: a mix of retro and modern, handmade and vintage, earnest and ironically hip.

Fitzroy is an eclectic neighborhood, full of galleries, indie boutiques, and artisan bakeries, and is dwarfed by huge Housing Commission high-rises across the park, where hundreds of low-income families live. Pip loves the neighborhood, but every day she sees families affected by substance abuse, a common problem in the area. "It seemed really important to try to get involved in some way without being negative or judgmental," she says. In 2007, she found out about the Mirabel Foundation, an organization that supports local families in need, and decided to rally the crafters she knew to make handmade softies for the children the foundation serves. "It seemed to me," she says, "that there were so very many children who really needed softies. Not just for their stitched-up beauty, but to have a special made-with-love friend to share their secrets with."

Pip used both her blog (www.meetmeatmikes.com), and her store window to get the word out about her Softies for Mirabel appeal. Meet Me at Mike's customers and crafters from all over the blogosphere responded to the call and began sending in their unique, handmade toys, everything from cats, dogs, and rabbits to llamas, platypuses, tarantulas, robots, monsters, and old-fashioned dolls wearing one-of-a-kind clothes. In 2007, the first year of the drive, Softies for Mirabel donated about 240 Christmas toys, "give or take a miscounted bunny."

Today, in addition to giving away the donated Softies, Pip auctions softies online to raise money for the foundation. When softies arrive by mail, from elsewhere in Australia, and from as far away as Finland and Brazil, Pip uploads photos of them to Flickr so that everyone can see them. Then, before delivering the toys to kids at Mirabel or mailing them to auction winners who might be anywhere in the world, Pip hangs them in the store window so that passersby can "see all the handmade goodness in the flesh." The amazing display of colorful, odd-looking creatures encourages even people who've never sewn before to join in the fun.

Pip hopes that Softies for Mirabel will continue to grow each year, but she wants the results of her work to remain concentrated and local. "For me," she says, "it's important to try and focus on one organization that means something to me and do as much as I can for that one group. I feel that I can have more impact that way." ✳

HOW YOU CAN HELP

Visit **www.meetmeatmikes.com** for guidelines and inspiration and to view the photo gallery of softies that have been donated in the past.

Make a softie and send it to:
Meet Me at Mike's
63 Brunswick Street
Fitzroy VIC 3065
Australia

Include your e-mail address, so that Meet Me at Mike's can let you know when your softie touches down.

Softies being donated to the Mirabel Christmas Appeal (those that go directly to children rather than auction) must not include buttons or other choking hazards.

If you are using someone else's softie pattern, contact the designer and ask for permission to reproduce it for this charity sale.

Mirabel the Owl

PATTERN DESIGNED BY SOFTIES FOR MIRABEL FOUNDER PIP LINCOLNE

A handmade toy makes a good confidante for a child who really needs a friend. Mirabel the Owl, originally designed to be auctioned for charity through Softies for Mirabel, can be pieced entirely from scraps of fabric and felt. Choose colors for her eyelids and beak that stand out against the felt you choose for her face. And be sure to give Mirabel lots of personality.

FINISHED SIZE
6 inches x 10 inches

WHAT YOU'LL NEED
Two 9-inch x 12-inch pieces of cotton fabric (or enough scraps to piece together two panels this size)

7-inch x 8-inch piece of wool felt (for face)

4-inch x 6-inch piece of wool felt (for eyelids)

2-inch x 3-inch piece of wool felt (for beak)

One sheet of double-sided, iron-on interfacing (for owl's features)

10 inches of jumbo rickrack or other trim

Mirabel the Owl template on page 86 (photocopy at 200 percent, then cut out the body, face, eyelid, and beak templates)

Small amount of polyfill toy stuffing

Black embroidery floss

Embroidery needle

Knitting needle or chopstick

Matching cotton thread

SEWING INSTRUCTIONS

1. Using the owl Body template, cut one body from each of the two 9-inch x 12-inch fabric panels, folding the panels in half vertically and placing the template's straight edge on the fabric's fold.

2. Trace the owl Face template on the interfacing. Cut out the face, peel off the paper on one side of the interfacing, and place the sticky side on the felt you're using for the face. Carefully cut around the interfacing.

3. Repeat step 2 using the templates and felt for both eyelids and for the beak.

4. Remove the paper backing from the interfaced felt face, and place the face on the body front, about ½ inch below the center top of the head. Use an iron to press the face and set the interfacing. Stitch around the face close to the edge, sewing either by hand (using matching cotton thread and a hand-sewing needle) or by machine.

5. Remove the paper backing from the eyelids, position them on the face, and press them in place. Edge-stitch (see page 130) around each eyelid, sewing by hand or by machine.

MIRABEL TEMPLATES

Photocopy at 200%

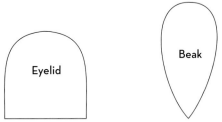

Eyelid

Beak

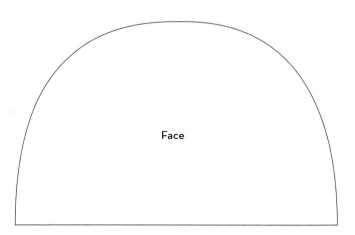

Face

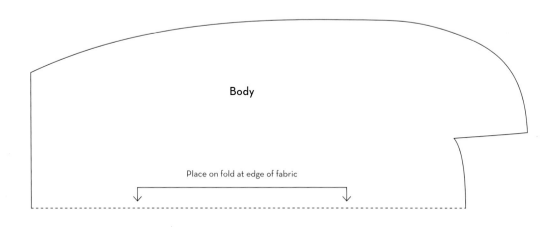

Body

Place on fold at edge of fabric

6. Using the black embroidery floss, embroider eyelashes at the base of each eyelid with long straight stitches.

7. Machine- or hand-sew the rickrack or other trim across the bottom of the owl's face. Then remove the paper backing from the beak, position and press it in place, and edge-stitch around it.

8. With the right sides together, align and sew the front body piece to the back body piece with a ¼-inch seam, leaving a several-inch opening for turning the owl right side out and stuffing it. To secure the seams, stitch over them a second time. Then turn the owl right side out, using a knitting needle or chopstick to fully turn out the owl's ears and corners.

9. Stuff the owl firmly with small pieces of stuffing, using a knitting needle or chopstick to work the stuffing into all the corners. Slipstitch (see page 131) the opening closed by hand.

Firehouse Quilts

In rural Colorado, firefighters are usually the first emergency crews to arrive at the scene of a fire, as you would expect. But they're often the first responders to car wrecks, outbursts of domestic violence, and other emergencies, as well. In almost a third of the state's fire districts, trucks leave the firehouses outfitted not only with tools and ladders, but also "snuggle quilts" made by the volunteers of Firehouse Quilts for the traumatized children firefighters might encounter.

Dusty Darrah, the founder of Firehouse Quilts, took up quilting soon after retiring from her job with the local phone company in 2001. At a quilting group she attended, she learned that members sometimes donated quilts to their local fire stations, and the firefighters would give them to children they encountered on their emergency runs. "I thought that was such a cool idea," Dusty says. She found out from a firefighter friend in nearby Littleton that her fire department didn't have a quilt program, so she started a group dedicated to making quilts for fire stations in communities throughout the foothills of the Rockies. Since then, Firehouse Quilts has grown into a nonprofit organization with more than fifty volunteers. The group donates quilts to fire stations across a wide swath of Colorado, as far east as the Kansas state line and up to Bailey and Conifer in the mountains to the west.

Dusty organizes two "sew days" a month in a long, light-filled room at the local rec center. About twenty-five to thirty volunteers come to each session. They're all women, although Dusty says, laughing, "We would accept men if they wanted to come." One of the sew days is actually a sew evening; the group meets in the early evening to accommodate members who work full-time and high school seniors fulfilling their community service requirement in order to graduate. To get the word out about the meetings, Dusty writes stories for the local newspaper about the firefighters who deliver the quilts and the kids who receive them. Sew days are friendly affairs, as much about socializing as quilting. Whenever a new volunteer shows up, Dusty assigns someone to sit with her and show her what to do. Plenty of people have learned to quilt for the first time at sew days. Whether volunteers make whole quilts out of precut kits or use their own patterns and fabric stashes, the process operates like an assembly line. Beginners cut and piece the quilt tops, experienced quilters do the quilting, often on professional long-arm machines, and a last set of volunteers squares up and binds the quilts.

Firehouse Quilts lets nothing go to waste. Volunteers collect coupons to use when they buy batting and other supplies. When local quilters pass away, their families often donate their fabric stashes to the organization. There's fabric at Dusty's house and at the houses of many volunteers. There's more in a closet at the rec center and at a self-storage unit in town. Dusty ends up dragging loads of fabric back and forth to the rec center along with all the sewing machines and other equipment. She's so tired of moving equipment and fabric around, that she's set a goal to find the group its own building. She'd also like to be able to offer free meeting space to other nonprofits struggling to get off the ground.

Dusty is committed to keeping Firehouse Quilts closely tied to the local community, so she has no plans to expand the group beyond Littleton, but she encourages other quilters to start copycat groups in their own communities. ✳

HOW YOU CAN HELP

Dusty Darrah worked with her local fire department to determine the perfect size for a quilt: 45 to 50 inches square, small enough to fold into a cubby hole in a fire truck cab, but big enough to comfort a good-size child.

Talk to your local fire chief before starting to make quilts to be sure that district rules allow the firehouses to participate. In rare cases, fire districts require extra paperwork when items are donated, and not all departments are willing to fill it out.

A group in England that donates quilts to emergency crews vacuum-packs them in plastic to save space in small ambulance cupboards.

Don't be afraid to ask your local community for what you need: fabric, publicity, space to sew in.

For more information on Firehouse Quilts, or for inspiration for starting your own quilting group, visit **www.firehousequilts.org**.

Emergency Snuggle Quilt

ADAPTED FROM A FIREHOUSE QUILTS PATTERN

This quilt was designed for first responders to give to children they encounter at emergency scenes. The Firehouse Quilts organization put a lot of thought into its size: small enough to fit into a cubbyhole in the cab of a fire truck, but big enough to help a frightened child feel safe. This version of the classic rail-fence pattern relies on a quick and easy strip-piecing method. You could piece a top on your own in a couple of hours or set up an assembly line with a few other quilters and make several.

FINISHED SIZE

Approximately 48 inches square

WHAT YOU'LL NEED

1 yard each of three contrasting 44-inch-wide quilting cottons (for quilt top)

3 yards of 44-inch-wide quilting cotton—you'll have some left over (for backing)

½ yard of one of the quilt top's darker fabrics (for binding)

Throw-size (60-inch-square) cotton batting

Matching cotton thread

SEWING INSTRUCTIONS

1. Choose one of your three quilt-top fabrics, and fold it lengthwise so that the selvedge edges are aligned. Then fold the fabric again lengthwise so that the fold line matches the two selvedge edges. You should now have a long four-layered rectangle of fabric 1 yard long and just over 10 inches wide. Using your rotary cutter and cutting mat, trim one of the folded fabric's short ends so that it is neat. Then cut ten 2¾-inch-deep strips. Trim the selvedge ends off each strip.

2. Repeat step 1 with the other two quilt-top fabrics.

3. With right sides together, sew together three strips, one from each fabric, side-by-side with ¼-inch seams. Press each seam's allowances together toward the darker fabric.

4. Cut the three-strip rectangle into five 7¼-inch squares.

5. Repeat steps 3 and 4 with the rest of the strips of fabric, being sure to keep the same fabric in the middle each time. You should end up with 50 squares. You'll use 49 of them and have one extra square (useful in case you make a mistake and need a spare).

6. Arrange the squares in seven rows of seven squares, rotating every other square 90 degrees to form a zigzag pattern.

7. Sew the squares into rows, aligning the long edges and using a ¼-inch seam. As you sew, match the edges of every block, pinching the two layers of fabric together at each intersection to keep the seams aligned until they reach your machine's presser foot. Press the seam allowances together to the darker side.

8. Sew the rows together, again matching the edges of every block.

9. Layer and pin-baste the quilt sandwich (see page 128).

10. Beginning at the center of the quilt and working out to the edge to prevent rippling, machine-quilt the sandwich with a grid or an allover meandering pattern (see page 130). Quilting continuous wavy lines along the "rails" is also a good option.

11. Bind the quilt with a traditional binding following the directions on page 129.

CHAPTER FOUR

Quilting to Change the World

Quilts can change the world. Or at least they can alter the opinions that shape the course of history. That was the hope behind the largest and most famous quilt ever made: the 1,293,300-square-foot, 54-ton AIDS Memorial Quilt. That quilt, which at this time commemorates more than 91,000 victims of HIV/AIDS, did indeed change the public's understanding of the disease and the basic human rights of its sufferers, which in turn provoked the U.S. government to act. In the United States alone, the quilt raised more than $4 million in donations for medical research and care. The disease might have claimed many, many more lives without that intervention of fabric, thread, sequins, and glue.

The AIDS Memorial Quilt was far from the first quilt designed to make a political or social statement. Before American women won the right to vote in 1920, they often stitched their positions into their quilts, whether they stood for or against a particular candidate or government policy. In the first decade of the twentieth century, for example, a quilt pattern was designed to support President Theodore Roosevelt's economic Square Deal. Other patterns, like Jacob's Ladder and Drunkard's Path, came to be associated with social causes from abolition to prohibition, and groups like the Woman's Christian Temperance Union raffled quilts to raise funds. It was no accident that Susan B. Anthony gave her first speech on women's suffrage at a quilting bee in Cleveland, Ohio.

In the 1980s, a number of quilting projects took on what was then the greatest threat to global peace and human life: the worldwide nuclear arms race. In 1985, for example, a project called The Ribbon wrapped the Pentagon and several national monuments in Washington, D.C., as well as the Atomic Bomb Dome in Hiroshima, Japan, in more than ten miles of quilt panels on the theme "What I cannot bear to think of as lost forever in a nuclear war." In the twenty-first century, the danger of nuclear proliferation has hardly disappeared, but climate change has joined it as an existential threat. A new generation of quilters has taken up needle and thread to raise awareness about the potentially devastating effects of global warming and to persuade others to act.

Not all quilted efforts on behalf of world peace are quite so vast in scale. Many projects, including those found in this chapter, tackle either the roots or the effects of suffering and conflict in smaller ways: by raising money to fight a specific disease, teaching children about human rights, establishing sustainable jobs in developing countries, or encouraging individuals to make small decisions that make a difference—like choosing shopping bags made of recycled fabric instead of plastic.

More Than Warmth

When the United States started bombing Afghanistan in 2001, quilter and peace activist Judy Meeker was teaching fourth grade at Granbery Elementary School in the suburbs of Nashville, Tennessee. She hadn't talked much with her students about the September 11 attacks or about the bombings because she wanted her classroom to be a "safe zone" where they could learn undisturbed by frightening world events. But when members of her quilting group suggested making quilts to send to Afghanistan, she recognized a great teaching opportunity—a positive, constructive way for the children to learn about what was happening overseas.

She gave the children squares of muslin and fabric markers and asked them to draw whatever would make them feel better if they were scared. No religious symbols or political images were allowed; no words, because a quilt bearing English words might endanger an Afghan family; and no pictures of helicopters, planes, or even rain—nothing to remind a child of the bombings. Instead, the children drew lots of animals (giraffes, for some reason, were a common theme), portraits of their families, and sunny outdoor scenes, often with rainbows and flowers. Jannah Shabazz, who was ten at the time, drew herself and a friend holding hands to show that "everybody could be friends and wouldn't hate each other." She told a local reporter, "Making quilts felt good, because my picture's on it, and they can look at my picture and know we're not bad people."

Every aspect of the quilt-making process was educational. The children learned to find Afghanistan on the map. They practiced geometry and multiplication as they planned the arrangement of the squares. They wrote letters to Afghan children to accompany the quilts. And they organized a fund-raiser to pay for the quilts to be finished by professional quilters. Judy found activists and aid workers willing to take the quilts to Afghanistan, and within six weeks, the quilts were in the hands of Afghan children.

The project became so popular that many other classes in the school took part. Even kindergarteners worked on quilts and discussed the war. "I told the kindergarteners they couldn't draw trucks, because soldiers were there in trucks," Judy says. "And of course, they all want to draw trucks at that point. I'd say, 'No you can't—we want to send pictures that don't scare the children.' It really got them to think." When discussing difficult subjects, Judy says, kids tend to be sensitive and attentive. "We go from such angst to 'Okay, now, would you like to bring hope to these people?' And they do."

An aid worker who had delivered quilts visited Judy's school soon after returning from Afghanistan. She told stories and showed photographs of the children who had received the quilts—some had been wounded or orphaned by the bombings. "It was pretty heavy and moving for my kids," Judy says. By then, she recognized how powerful the quilts could be, both for the children who made them and those who received them. When the school year ended in mid-2002, she quit her job and devoted herself full-time to teaching quilting workshops and developing materials to help other teachers use quilting to teach their students about the consequences of war and poverty for children. She started a nonprofit organization, More Than Warmth, and launched a website and regular e-mail newsletter as a way of reaching as many teachers as she could. Today

Judy travels around the country, visiting schools as an artist-in-residence, and holding workshops to train teachers in her methods. She also works on building her network of aid workers, diplomats, and local agencies to help her distribute quilts in developing countries and war zones around the world.

Well over 13,000 children around the United States have participated in quilt-making projects through More Than Warmth. Quilts have been sent to former child soldiers in Africa and to boys rescued from slavery in India. They've been given to pregnant women in Baghdad and Iraqi refugees in Jordan. They've gone to Iran, Swaziland, North Korea, Mexico, Tibet, Israel, China, Thailand, Sudan—forty-five countries in all.

Judy sometimes tells students that during the Underground Railroad, messages directing slaves to freedom may have been embedded in quilts. "It's much the same as what we're doing," she says. "We're designing messages to pass on to people in Fallujah and Baghdad and Africa." The quilts are full of the children's attention, and their recipients feel that, Judy says. She gives the example of the boys freed from slavery in Indian rug factories. "For years, they feel lost. When they realize someone cares, it's really important to them. Just that a child in America would learn about them is momentous." ✳

HOW YOU CAN HELP

If you are a teacher or youth group leader, conduct a More Than Warmth quilt-making workshop with your students. Go to www.morethanwarmth.org for guidelines.

Donate cotton fabric or make a monetary donation to More Than Warmth to sponsor a classroom quilt-making project or to help defray the costs of shipping quilts internationally.

If you are traveling to a poverty-stricken or war-torn country, consider carrying a few quilts with you.

For more information about these opportunities, send an e-mail to info@morethanwarmth.org.

eQuilter.com

Jean Lafitte, Louisiana, a small fishing community on the west bank of the Mississippi, survived Hurricane Katrina in 2005 with relatively little damage. But a month later, Hurricane Rita devastated the town. Kathy Price, the force behind a tiny Ohio-based nonprofit aid organization called Mission of Love, was helping with the rescue effort in New Orleans when she heard how desperately Jean Lafitte's residents needed help. "As in most disasters," she said, "all the aid goes to the center, while the outlying people, the really poor, are always excluded." Kathy and her husband, Bob, drove directly to Jean Lafitte with medical supplies, food, and water. About two months later, they returned to deliver handmade quilts and other gifts, and the following year they rebuilt seven houses in Jean Lafitte. They did all this largely through the generosity of quilters, in particular one named Luana Rubin, founder of eQuilter.com.

Luana and her husband, Paul, started an online fabric business in the basement of their Boulder, Colorado, home in 1999. From the very beginning, they incorporated philanthropy into their business plan. Currently the largest quilting store on the web, eQuilter now occupies a 15,000-square-foot warehouse, employs thirty-seven people, and maintains an inventory of more than 20,000 products. Two percent of the company's revenues go directly to charities like the hurricane cleanup efforts. Whenever a customer places an order, she or he can choose the destination of that 2 percent from a carefully vetted list of nonprofits. The company has given more than $600,000 and thousands of handmade quilts to organizations ranging from Doctors Without Borders and the National Breast Cancer Foundation to the Rainforest Action Network, the Ocean Conservancy, and, of course, Mission of Love.

These contributions had been mainly monetary until September 11, 2001, when eQuilter was inundated by e-mails from customers who wanted to make quilts for survivors and the families of those who had died. "We said, 'Okay, send it to us, and we will guarantee it will get to somebody who needs it,'" Luana recalls. She was in an ideal position to coordinate quilters' efforts: She had warehouse space, the e-mail addresses of tens of thousands of quilters, and—thanks to her years of fund-raising for nonprofits—contacts at organizations assisting survivors and bereaved families. Within a few months, a pastor Luana knew had distributed 700 quilts made by eQuilter customers for survivors. And on the first anniversary of September 11, Mission of Love delivered a truckload of quilts to a New York neighborhood where the families of some of the attacks' poorest victims lived.

"Some quilters will put their name and their contact information on the back of the quilt, and they will feel a little funny if they don't get some kind of response back from the person who received it," Luana says. "But sometimes the best way to give is when you know it's going to people who can't respond, because they're in such a bad situation. When you are distributing quilts to people who are horribly traumatized, you have to go into it with an open heart. You have to think, 'I would like to give this gift, and I trust that it's going to go to the right person.' When you donate a quilt, you really just have to let it go." That's why Luana so carefully researches the organizations she works with—to be sure the quilts her customers make will reach the people who need them most. As the mother of an adopted child from China, she is particularly interested in helping orphans around the world. She has worked with Altrusa International to distribute quilts and funding to orphanages in the Chinese province of Jiangxi, and with Quilts Beyond Borders, an effort to collect hundreds of handmade quilts for Ethiopian children orphaned by HIV/AIDS.

Since 2001, Luana has used the weekly e-mail newsletter she sends out to her customers to rally volunteers to make quilts and send donations following a variety of disasters and emergencies. For example, one time she asked for quilts for a small orphanage that had burned down on the Pine Ridge Reservation in South Dakota; another time, she asked for donations to buy coal, disposable diapers, warm clothes and snow boots for orphanages in south and central China when unusually heavy snowstorms knocked out power and transportation. In the wake of a disaster of any size, speed is of the essence, Luana says.

Though the quilts may be made quickly and put to use in temporary shelters, there's nothing temporary about their effect. Kathy of Mission of Love, who has personally delivered hundreds of the handmade quilts collected by eQuilter, says, "They are such a gift to the people on the other end, because they know the work and time and love that go into each and every stitch. Because there aren't many things that are handmade anymore, they will cherish them." ✳

HOW YOU CAN HELP

When you purchase fabric and supplies at the eQuilter website, 2 percent of the proceeds is donated to a charity that you pick from a list of options. You can also sign up for Luana's weekly newsletters at www.equilter.com, which call for quilts in response to a variety of disasters. The newsletters describe the specifics of what is appropriate for each situation. Typically, it is important that the quilt can be made quickly.

Speedy Housetop Quilt

In the wake of a disaster, people need basic necessities like bedding fast. As Luana Rubin of eQuilter.com says, "Just do something that you can actually finish and finish quickly, and that's not going to cost an arm or a leg to ship." This quilt fits those requirements. It doesn't take long to cut or piece, and you can finish it in just a day. The housetop pattern is extremely simple—you start with a square and build outward from that.

FINISHED SIZE
70 inches x 90 inches

WHAT YOU'LL NEED
For quilt top
¾ yard of 44-inch-wide quilting cotton in large-scale floral print (Fabric 1)

1 yard each of 44-inch-wide quilting cotton in two solid colors (Fabrics 2 and 3)

1¼ yards of 44-inch-wide quilting cotton in third solid color (Fabric 4)

1¼ yards of 44-inch-wide quilting cotton in fourth solid color (Fabric 5)

1½ yards of 44-inch-wide quilting cotton in small-scale print (Fabric 6)

For backing
5½ yards of 44-inch-wide quilting cotton

Full-sized (93 inches x 96 inches) cotton batting

Matching cotton thread

SEWING INSTRUCTIONS
1. Cut a 20-inch square from Fabric 1.

2. From the remaining fabrics, cut the following selvedge-to-selvedge strips, and trim the selvedge ends on each strip.

   Fabric 2: Two 5-inch-wide strips and two 7½-inch-wide strips

   Fabric 3: Three 5-inch-wide strips and two 7½-inch-wide strips

   Fabric 4: Three 5-inch-wide strips and three 7½-inch-wide strips

   Fabric 5: Four 5-inch-wide strips and three 7½-inch-wide strips

   Fabric 6: Four 5-inch-wide strips and four 7½-inch-wide strips.

3. With right sides together and the edges aligned, sew one 7½-inch-wide strip of Fabric 2 to one side of the 20-inch square. Press the seam's allowances toward the darker fabric. Trim the ends of the strip even with the edges of the square. (Note that each time you join a strip in the following steps, you will press the seam allowances toward the darker fabric and trim the ends this way.)

4. Moving clockwise and with right sides together and the edges aligned, sew one 5-inch-wide strip of Fabric 2 to the long side of the rectangle formed by the square and first strip.

5. Again turn the pieced rectangle 90 degrees clockwise, sew the second 7½-inch-wide strip of Fabric 2 to the side formed by the square and second strip.

6. Sew the second 5-inch-wide strip of Fabric 2 to the side of the rectangle formed by the square and the ends of both 7½-inch strips.

7. Turn the pieced rectangle 90 degrees clockwise, and add one 7½-inch-wide strip of Fabric 3 to the new side.

Turn the rectangle 90 degrees, add one 5-inch-wide strip of Fabric 3. Turn again, add one 7½-inch-wide strip.

For the fourth side, you'll need to piece two 5-inch strips end to end to create a strip long enough to span this side.

8. Continue to turn the quilt top clockwise 90 degrees, adding 7½-inch strips to the top and bottom and 5-inch strips to both sides, piecing the strips as needed for length to form concentric rectangles around the center square in Fabrics 4, 5, and 6 (see Diagram A).

9. Make a quilt sandwich, and pin-baste it in place (see page 128).

10. Here are two options for machine-quilting this quilt:

    A. Lower the feed dogs on your machine, and replace your regular presser foot with a darning foot if you have one (if you don't, lower the feed dogs and proceed with your regular presser foot).

Starting in the center square and moving out toward the edge of the quilt, stitch freestyle rectangles in various sizes, joining each rectangle to the next with a line (see Diagram B) and not worrying if the corners of your rectangles aren't sharp. Cover the entire quilt with connected rectangles.

    B. Use a walking foot on your machine if you have one (don't worry if you don't have one; your regular presser foot will also work fine). At the center of the quilt, mark a 5-inch square; then mark concentric squares at 2-inch intervals using a quilter's rule and a chalk marking pen. When you reach the outside edge of the center square, begin marking rectangles that echo the pieced "frames" that surround it. Starting in the center and working out, stitch along the marked lines.

11. Bind the quilt with a mock binding following the directions on page 130.

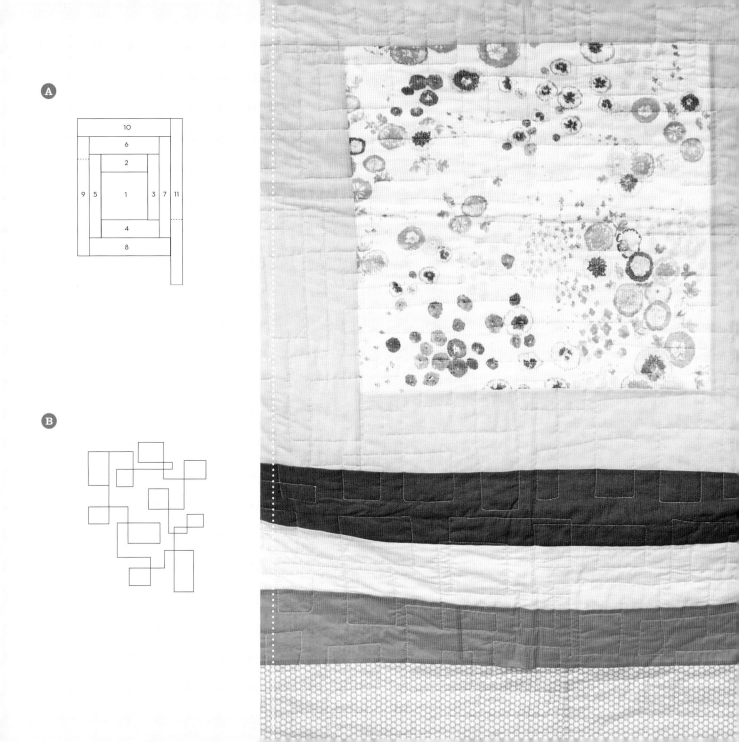

A

| | 10 | |
| 6 |
| 2 |
| 9 | 5 | 1 | 3 | 7 | 11 |
| 4 |
| 8 |

B

Vietnam Quilts

Patchwork quilts are an iconic part of American culture, but there's a long history of both patchwork and quilting in many other countries as well. As early as the eighteenth century, patterns, techniques, and fabric were exchanged along trade routes and carried back and forth by missionaries and other travelers. You can see Welsh influence in nineteenth-century Pennsylvania Amish designs, American log cabin patterns in antique pieced-silk wrapping cloths in Korea, and Japanese fabrics in contemporary American quilts. And in twenty-first-century Vietnam, an enterprising quilter has combined local fabrics and sewing skills with an international design sensibility to create an innovative rural development project.

Thanh Truong, a dentist from Vietnam, learned to quilt while living in Europe. She returned to Vietnam in 1994, after eighteen years in France, because she and her husband wanted to help people living in poverty there. As she traveled around Binh Thuan province, about a four-hour drive northeast of Ho Chi Minh City, Thanh saw few good long-term employment opportunities for rural women. Many women traveled to harvest cassava and cashews in faraway fields—unstable, seasonal work that sometimes forced them to leave their children alone for days at a time. Thanh believed that patchwork would be an ideal form of employment for the women. It's labor-intensive, but it doesn't require much infrastructure and would allow them to work locally—making child care easier—and in comfortable conditions.

In 2001, under the auspices of Vietnam Plus, a small French and Belgian nonprofit development organization (Thanh's husband, Bernard, is its director), Thanh launched Vietnam Quilts. With the help of an American quilter, Stacey Newsbury, who was teaching English in Vietnam, Thanh trained thirteen women in patchwork, hand- and machine-quilting, and appliqué. At first, the quilts were sold Tupperware-party-style in the homes of foreigners living in Vietnam. Profits went to fund local development projects.

Thanh's next step was to open a retail quilt shop in Ho Chi Minh City. The store's first location, next to a smelly canal, made it difficult to attract customers. After Thanh reopened the shop in District 1, the city center, business grew faster, allowing her to establish six more quilting groups in Binh Thuan province, another two in the Mekong Delta, and a second shop in Hanoi. Vietnam Quilts now employs nearly 200 women who make about 360 quilts a month. Vietnam Quilts is always looking for ways to sell more quilts, in order to employ more women. In addition to the shops, the organization sells quilts on its website (www.vietnam-quilts.org) and is currently exploring opportunities for exporting overseas. For that plan to work, says Lisa Owen, an Australian who volunteers as sales and marketing manager at the Ho Chi Minh City store, it's essential that potential partners understand that Vietnam Quilts can never compete with producers who don't pay workers a fair wage.

Most women who work for Vietnam Quilts have doubled their families' incomes and begun saving for the first time. A former day laborer named Ngoc, for example, has earned enough to pay for treatment for her sick child, build a proper latrine, and buy iron sheets to make a roof for her open-air kitchen; she also received a loan so she could begin raising pigs. The quilters' wages are adjusted regularly for inflation, they receive health insurance and maternity and bereavement payments, and Vietnam Plus workers visit weekly to ensure that working conditions remain at a high standard. All profits continue to be reinvested into the communities, supporting scholarships for children from extremely poor families, health education, and other programs.

By the end of a six-month training session, the women have become expert quilters. Each group leader visits Ho Chi Minh City or Hanoi monthly to deliver quilts, find out about new designs, and pick up new material. A production manager checks each quilt to be sure the craftsmanship is up to Vietnam Quilts' exacting standards. At both stores, volunteers—including expats, locals, and visitors, usually from France or Australia—help with sales, marketing, and quilt design.

While Vietnam has a long history of patchwork quilting, Vietnamese quilts were traditionally rather humble and utilitarian, Lisa Owen says. "It was largely taken up by the poor, or by people experiencing financial hardship. Small scraps of fabric were pieced together to make blankets for purely practical purposes. They were not created with any intentional aesthetic appeal." A visit to Vietnam Quilts' Ho Chi Minh City shop, however, tells a new story. The quilts are gorgeous, varied, and anything but utilitarian: intricately stitched whole cloth quilts, bright baby quilts, quilts pieced in traditional American and European patterns, and contemporary Asian quilts bearing lotuses and pineapples. Some of the most popular are Vietnam Quilts' reinterpretations of classic patterns, like the American sunbonnet girl of the 1930s. In the Vietnamese version, the little appliquéd girls are dressed not in pinafores and sunbonnets, but in *ao dais* (long dresses over pants) and traditional conical hats. It's a fitting motif for the cross-cultural exchange that's been so crucial to Vietnam Quilts' success. ✳

HOW YOU CAN HELP

Support Vietnam Quilts' efforts to raise the quality of life for women and their families in rural Vietnam by purchasing a quilt at Vietnam Quilts' online shop: www.vietnam-quilts.org.

If you are planning to travel to Vietnam, contact the shops and ask about volunteering.

Ho Chi Minh City:
vietnam.quilts.hcm@gmail.com

Hanoi:
vietnam.quilts.hn@gmail.com

Morsbags

Claire Morsman lives on a barge on the Grand Union Canal in West London. After growing up near the sea in southwest England, she never likes to be too far from the water, but there's one drawback to her living situation—she's frequently disturbed by the number of discarded plastic bags floating past on the canal.

Globally, more than a million plastic bags are used per minute, and a huge number of these end up in the ocean, where they do untold damage to marine wildlife, especially when they are mistaken for food. When Claire researched the effects of plastic bags on sea creatures, she was horrified to discover a photograph of a tangle of bags removed from the stomach of a young minke whale that had washed up on a beach in Normandy, France. "I decided I could do something simple and immediate," she says, "to personally not accept plastic bags from shops anymore by making my own from spare material."

Claire, then thirty-one, had only sewn in a home economics course at school, so she asked her mother for help designing a super-simple bag pattern. Her idea took off from there. "I realized that if I could make them, why couldn't everyone else?" she says. "I decided to put the pattern online so that everybody could help themselves and make their own bags." Claire wanted an original, memorable name for the bags—"green bags" and "eco bags" were already too common—so she used part of her own name. Her fiancé, Joseph, designed the Morsbags website. From there, the project grew by word of mouth—both online and off.

What's brilliant about Morsbags is that it makes doing something constructive about an enormous and depressing problem not only easy, but a lot of fun. Claire describes it as a "sociable guerrilla" operation. Morsbaggers organize into local "pods" of volunteers, who get together, share wine and/or dessert, and make as many bags as they can in an evening. More experienced sewers sometimes add flourishes to the bags—pockets, patchwork, quilting—but a basic bag takes less than half an hour to complete (fifteen minutes if the baggers arrange themselves into mini production lines). Almost all of the fabric is reclaimed from old clothes and bedding, so material that otherwise might be thrown away is kept out of landfills, and new material doesn't need to be produced in order to make the bags. As most fabric production involves lots of harmful pesticides and water, not to mention the fuel used in transporting it from factory to warehouse to shop, Morsbags help the environment in multiple ways. They're also a great way for quilters to use up scraps left over from other projects.

Once Morsbaggers amass a quantity of bags, they organize "guerrilla handouts" at local supermarkets, where they give bags to unsuspecting shoppers on their way inside. "Most people are surprised and thrilled to accept a free, handmade, useful, and unique gift," Claire says, "but for a few there's always the suspicion of 'What's the catch?' and 'What are they trying to sell?' Once we've explained the idea behind Morsbags to the less easily convinced people, there's a certain thawing and they tend to go away enthusiastic and converted." When shy Morsbaggers don't feel comfortable distributing bags to strangers, she encourages them to give bags to friends, family, neighbors, and coworkers. Volunteers always sew labels onto the bags they give away, hoping that recipients will visit the website and begin sewing Morsbags themselves.

Morsbags has become a worldwide movement, with about 2,000 volunteers. The majority live in the United Kingdom and the United States, but Claire knows of groups or individuals making Morsbags in countries all over the globe, including New Zealand, Bulgaria, Japan, Egypt, Abu Dhabi, India, Thailand, Singapore, Columbia, and the Philippines.

At last count, Morsbaggers had made nearly 27,000 bags, potentially replacing more than 13 million plastic bags. "Small actions by individuals really count," Claire says. ✺

HOW YOU CAN HELP

Make cloth shopping bags using the instructions on page 106 or on the Morsbags website, and give them away.

Go to **www.morsbags.com** to find a "pod" of others near you who make Morsbags, or start a group of your own.

30-Minute Shopping Bag

ADAPTED FROM THE MORSBAGS PATTERN

Use recycled fabric or leftover scraps from quilting projects to make this bag extra eco-friendly. If you want to use small scraps of fabric, read the patchwork instructions at the end of the pattern. Double seams make the bag more durable for heavy groceries, giving it a longer life.

FINISHED SIZE

Approximately 15¾ inches x 16¾ inches

WHAT YOU'LL NEED

¾ yard of 44-inch-wide quilting- or home decorating-weight cotton (preferably recycled)

Knitting needle or chopstick

Matching cotton thread

SEWING INSTRUCTIONS

1. Cut two 18-inch x 20-inch pieces of fabric for the front and back of the shopping bag, and two 18-inch x 4-inch strips for the handles.

2. Fold and press a ½-inch hem on one long edge of one handle strip. Fold and press a 1-inch hem on the opposite long edge of this handle strip. Fold and press the side with the narrow hem so it overlaps the side with the wide hem by ½ inch (see Diagram A).

3. Edge-stitch (see page 130) the edge of the overlapped hem, and then topstitch (see page 131) ¼ inch on either side of the first seam.

4. Repeat steps 2-3 to make the second handle.

5. Working with one of the 18-inch x 20-inch rectangles, fold and press to the wrong side a ½-inch hem on one short end. Fold and press this hem edge another 1½ inches to the wrong side. Next position each end of one handle 4½ inches from each side edge of the rectangle and tuck the handle ends under the double-folded hem, snugging them to the base of the hem (the handle will now face into the center of the rectangle), as shown in Diagram B.

Pin the double-folded hem and handle ends in place, and edge-stitch as close to the edge of the hem as you can, taking out the pins as you come to them.

Fold the handle up over the hem, and press it in place (see Diagram C).

6. Topstitch a box with an X inside it on each end of the handle, covering the bag's hem (see Diagram D).

7. Repeat steps 2-6 with the second fabric rectangle and handle.

8. Place the bag's two sides with wrong sides together and the edges aligned. Sew a ¼-inch seam along both sides and the bottom of the bag, backstitching (see page 130) at the beginning and end of the seam

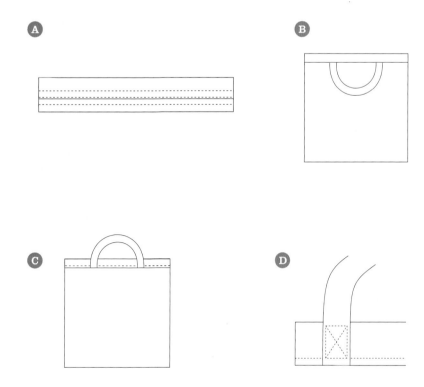

to secure it. Turn the bag wrong side out, using a knitting needle or chopstick to gently push the corners fully out. Press the bag's edges, and, with a ½-inch seam, sew around the three closed sides, again backstitching at the beginning and end of your stitching. Trim any loose threads, turn the bag right side out, and press it again.

Patchwork variation

Piece together strips or scraps of fabric, and trim your patchwork to create the two 18-inch x 20-inch rectangles. Then follow steps 1-8 above to make your shopping bag.

The AIDS
Memorial Quilt

In 1952, an Indiana quilter named Irene Rupert made a crazy quilt. She cut some of the patches from the linings of her husband's smoking jacket, his bathrobe, and his pajamas, and along the seams she quilted an intricate decorative stitch. She gave the quilt to her grandson Cleve Jones, who was born in 1954. "It was a good quilt for a little boy," Cleve says. During his childhood, it became to him a symbol of family and continuity; he has kept it to this day.

In his early twenties, Cleve moved to San Francisco and joined the gay liberation movement. He became friends with city supervisor and gay rights activist Harvey Milk and went to work in his office as an intern. Eleven months later, on November 27, 1978, Milk was shot and killed, along with George Moscone, the mayor. Tens of thousands of grieving people marched by candlelight down San Francisco's Market Street from the Castro, where most of the city's gay population lived, toward City Hall.

For years afterward, Cleve organized a candlelight march every November 27 to commemorate Harvey Milk and George Moscone. In 1985, as he was preparing for the march, he read a shocking newspaper headline: One thousand San Franciscans had died of the new disease, HIV/AIDS.

"I was standing at the corner of Castro and Market when I read that headline," Cleve says, "and was very conscious that of those first thousand, almost all had lived and died within a few blocks, literally, of where I was standing." As people gathered for that year's march, he asked them to write on placards the names of their friends who had died of AIDS. When the march was over, Cleve and other activists leaned extension ladders on the Federal building, climbed three stories up, and taped the placards to the wall. Cleve remembers:

I thought to myself, it looks like some strange quilt. I immediately thought of my grandmother and great-grandmother, and it was such a powerful symbol of family love and family loyalty. I had this vision in my head of the National Mall covered with a giant quilt. To me, it worked immediately on so many levels. There was the tradition of quilting itself, of taking fabrics of different texture and color and creating a unified whole out of many pieces. It was about valuing everything and everyone, not wasting fabric or lives. I could see it working as therapy. I had a picture in my head of families deep in grief for the loss of a loved one sitting on their living-room floor with scissors and thread and fabric and glue. I saw it as a tool for the media, which at that time was obsessed with statistics and paid no attention to the lives that were behind the statistics. I thought it could be a weapon to direct at the government, to shame the politicians with this incredible visual symbol of the consequences of their failure to act.

Many people thought Cleve's idea wouldn't work. They told him it was too morbid and sentimental, and they didn't think people would participate. "I knew they would," Cleve says. "That's the part I never doubted, because people were so lost and becoming paralyzed with grief, and something like this was so urgently needed."

In 1987, Cleve's newly incorporated Names Project Foundation opened a storefront workshop on San Francisco's Market Street. A handwritten sign on the window asked for help in the form of volunteers, fabric and thread, sewing machines, office supplies, back rubs, and lemonade. Neighbors ransacked their closets and brought armfuls of fabric. People came together in the workshop to sew and grieve, often staying until three in the morning. "The workshop was a magic place," Cleve says. "All of us cried every day, but there was also a lot of laughter and great beauty. When we started that project, our hearts were full of hate and fear and despair. We hated the straight world for abandoning us, and we were very frightened of the illness we knew that most of us would face. There was no treatment, there was no action by the government. But the quilt, and the people we met through the quilt, turned all of that into love and courage and hope."

Each panel of the AIDS Memorial Quilt measures three by six feet, roughly the size of a grave, and each contributor is encouraged to make the panel personal, using both traditional and nontraditional materials that represent the individual being remembered. Cleve made the first panel himself, for his best friend, Marvin Feldman. An experienced quilter from across the bay in Berkeley, Nancy Katz, helped him conceive the way the panels would fit together into a quilt. Eight panels were sewn into a twelve-foot square. For many displays, nine squares formed a huge, but otherwise traditional, nine-patch block. When the AIDS Memorial Quilt

> **66**
>
> Never doubt that a small group of thoughtful, committed citizens can change the world. Indeed, it is the only thing that ever has.
>
> **99**
>
> MARGARET MEAD

MATERIALS USED IN THE AIDS MEMORIAL QUILT

100-year-old quilt, afghans, Barbie dolls, bubble wrap, burlap, buttons, car keys, carpet, champagne glasses, condoms, cookies, corduroy, corsets, cowboy boots, cremation ashes, credit cards, curtains, dresses, feather boas, first-place ribbons, fishnet hose, flags, flip-flops, fur, gloves, hats, human hair, jeans, jewelry, jockstraps, lace, lamé, leather, Lego blocks, love letters, Mardi Gras masks, merit badges, mink, motorcycle jackets, needlepoint, paintings, pearls, photographs, pins, plastic, police uniforms, quartz crystals, racing silks, records, rhinestones, sequins, shirts, silk flowers, studs, stuffed animals, suede, t-shirts, taffeta, tennis shoes, vinyl, wedding rings.

was displayed for the first time in October 1987, at the march on Washington for lesbian and gay rights, it included 1,920 panels and covered an area bigger than a football field. During an opening ceremony that would be repeated at every major display, eight people unfolded each elaborately folded square, while the names of the dead were read aloud. They lifted the quilt to let it billow and settle onto a square of white canvas laid onto the ground. It looked, Cleve says, like an ordinary quilt billowing and settling onto a newly made bed. The canvas formed walkways among the squares.

After the first display on the Mall, Cleve bought a truck, named it Stella, and began touring the country with the quilt. Chapters of the Names Project were established all over the United States. As the years wore on, thousands and thousands of people—gay and straight, conservative and liberal, people who had little in common but the fact that they had lost loved ones to the disease—sent panels to San Francisco or to their local Names Project chapters. Many people's contributions to the quilt were made in secret, as it was still very difficult to come out as a gay man in many parts of the country. In Pittsburgh in 1989, for example, a young man approached Nancy Howard, an accomplished quilter and quilting teacher, and commissioned a quilt for a friend. He told her it had to be three feet by six feet, and he wanted his friend's name spelled out across it. He didn't explain why he wanted the quilt made, and Nancy, who by her own admission was rather naïve in those days, didn't guess. Two years later, when the AIDS Memorial Quilt came to Pittsburgh, Nancy understood. She went to see the quilt, and among hundreds of panels found the one she had made.

During the worst of the epidemic in the United States, the quilt was displayed every year on the National Mall, until it grew too large to appear all at once. Since then, it has never stopped growing (it included more than 40,000 panels at last count), and the idea has been taken up in many other countries. To date, more than 18 million people have seen the quilt displayed, and the Names Project Foundation has raised over $4 million in donations for services for people with HIV/AIDS.

The original AIDS Memorial Quilt could only have been created in the Castro, Cleve says, because the effects of the epidemic were so immediate, so personal, and so concentrated there. But he had imagined the quilt with not only his fellow San Franciscans in mind, but also his Midwestern family. He knew that while thousands of gay men suffered from the disease and the isolation and shame that came with it, their families were also struggling with the stigma, along with their grief. The quilt was designed to bring many of those people together, to make HIV/AIDS a topic of mainstream discussion and concern, and to broaden the political struggle for funding for research and treatment. The quilt accomplished that and much more. "There's no doubt in my mind," Cleve says, "that the quilt had a profound impact on our culture and this country's response to AIDS. So much of what the lesbian, gay, bisexual, and transgender community has achieved recently comes out of the epidemic. People saw us dying, but they also saw us caring for our partners and our friends. They saw the rejection we experienced. Once people were exposed to the reality of it, it was impossible for most of them not to be moved." ✳

HOW YOU CAN HELP

Make a 3-foot x 6-foot panel to commemorate the life of someone you know who has died of AIDS. Use a design and materials that represent the individual being remembered.

Fill out a panelmaker information form on the AIDS Quilt website (listed below) and send it with your quilt panel to: The Names Project Foundation 637 Hoke St. NW Atlanta, GA 30318-4315

Help others sew panels at a panel-making workshop in your area. To find contact information for your local Names Project chapter, to learn more about volunteering, and to find out where the exhibit is being displayed, visit **www.aidsquilt.org**.

Alzheimer's Art Quilt Initiative

Beebe Moss, a painter, started quilting in her seventies. "Mom never did anything the 'right' way," her daughter Ami Simms says. "She was very creative and ignored directions. Rather than cut patches, assemble them in rows, and then sew the rows together, she sewed patches together circularly, or randomly." When Beebe was diagnosed with Alzheimer's in 2001, she moved in with Ami and her husband in Flint, Michigan, so that they could take care of her.

Ami, a successful quilt artist and quilting teacher, devised projects to keep her mother busy as her Alzheimer's advanced. Beebe hand-stamped and hand-dyed fabric, painted note cards, and made pieces of freestyle patchwork. Whenever Ami taught quilting, she asked her students to turn her mother's fabric and patchwork into quilts to donate to any charity they pleased.

"People would send us pictures of quilts they'd finished using her fabric or patchwork," she says. "Most of the time, she never recognized it as anything she'd created." The progression of her disease was evident in her paintings, too—over time, they lost detail and became more and more abstract until they seemed to hold no meaning at all.

In 2005, after her mother had moved into a special care facility, Ami decided to make a quilt about Alzheimer's. "It wasn't going to be pretty," she says. "I wanted to take some of Mom's patchwork—with the mismatched seams, holes, and pleats—and machine-quilt it with black thread. I wanted my anger to flow into that thread and just pummel the quilt with the needle." Making that small, angry quilt was a cathartic experience for Ami. It also gave her the idea for the Alzheimer's Art Quilt Initiative, "an Internet-driven grassroots, totally volunteer effort to raise awareness and fund research through art."

For the Initiative's first project, Ami organized "Alzheimer's: Forgetting Piece by Piece," a traveling exhibit of fifty-two art quilts, many by internationally renowned artists, to raise awareness about the disease. Many of the quilts were made by quilt artists and teachers Ami knew; a jury chose the rest. The quilts express their makers' meditations on the effects of Alzheimer's on its sufferers and their loved ones. Ami's own contribution includes an old-fashioned patchwork house, fabric printed with Ami's recollections of things her mother said and did, and a photo transfer of a burned electric cord. In an oral history of the project recorded in 2007, Ami said, "The name of the quilt is 'Underlying Current,' and that motif of the electrical current running through the quilt physically is to symbolize the feeling of having that constant stress and pressure on a caregiver for caring for someone who has a chronic or a fatal disease, because it is always there when you are responsible for another who cannot take care of themselves." Since August 2006, more than 200,000 people have visited the exhibit at quilt shows and museums in twenty-five states.

Another Alzheimer's Art Quilt Initiative project raises funds for medical research. Quilters of all different persuasions and ability levels create "priority quilts"—miniature quilts small enough to fit into a nine-inch-by-twelve-inch priority mail envelope—and each month, Ami auctions them online, earning anywhere from $5 to $350 per little quilt. Dedicated quilters sign up for the $1000 Promise, pledging to make and donate enough quilts to raise $1000. The quilts (more than 3,000 of them so far) vary wildly, from personal reflections on loved ones lost to Alzheimer's to experiments with techniques, patterns, and materials to miniature versions of traditional quilts. Many quilters who donate priority quilts have some connection to the disease, but others simply want to help and enjoy making small, creative projects. "It's a great way," Ami says, "to try out a new technique or perfect an old one, experiment with colors you ordinarily wouldn't use, finish up orphan blocks and old workshop projects, or go way out on a limb and work outside your comfort level. We're talking not a lot of time investment, which makes risk-taking much easier."

The quilts may be tiny, but their impact has been huge. At the time of this writing, they have raised nearly $200,000 for Alzheimer's research. ✳

HOW YOU CAN HELP

Make a Priority Alzheimer's Quilt using the instructions on page 114. Go to www.alzquilts.org to register your quilt. You'll receive an email with instructions on how and where to send your quilt. You can also sign up on the website to become a $1,000 Promise quilter, pledging to make enough Priority Quilts to raise $1,000.

Buy a Priority Alzheimer's Quilt, available for auction at the website listed above.

Priority Alzheimer's Quilt

"FAST-FINISH TRIANGLES" DESIGN BY TERRY SWITZER CHILKO; BINDING TECHNIQUE
FROM THE ALZHEIMER'S ART QUILT INITIATIVE

When making a "priority quilt" to donate to the Alzheimer's Art Quilt Initiative, you can design and quilt it however you like, as long as it fits inside a Priority Mail envelope. I made a postage-stamp quilt to continue the postal theme, but feel free to experiment. Simply make a quilt sandwich no bigger than 9 inches x 12 inches, and then follow steps 10 through 24 to bind and prepare your quilt for hanging on the wall.

FINISHED SIZE
9 inches x 11 inches

WHAT YOU'LL NEED
12-inch x 4-inch pieces of quilting cotton in each of 8 small prints and solids (for quilt top)

10-inch x 12-inch piece of quilting cotton (for backing)

Four 3¾-inch squares of quilting cotton (for Fast-Finish Triangles)

1¾-inch-deep, selvedge-to-selvedge strip of 44-inch-wide quilting cotton (for binding)

10-inch x 12-inch piece of cotton batting

Curved quilter's safety pins

Matching cotton thread

Two dowels or chopsticks (for hanging quilt)

SEWING INSTRUCTIONS

1. From your various 12-inch x 4-inch pieces of cotton, randomly cut sixty-three 1¾-inch squares.

2. Arrange and rearrange the squares in seven rows of nine squares until you're satisfied with the distribution of colors and prints.

3. With right sides together and aligning the edges of each pair of squares being joined to form a row, sew the squares into seven rows using ¼-inch seams.

4. With right sides together and the edges aligned, sew the rows together with ¼-inch seams to form the quilt top, matching the corners of the squares as you work.

5. Square up the quilt top (see page 132).

6. Layer the backing, batting, and quilt top to form a quilt sandwich (see page 128).

7. Pin the layers together using curved quilter's safety pins spaced about 3 inches apart.

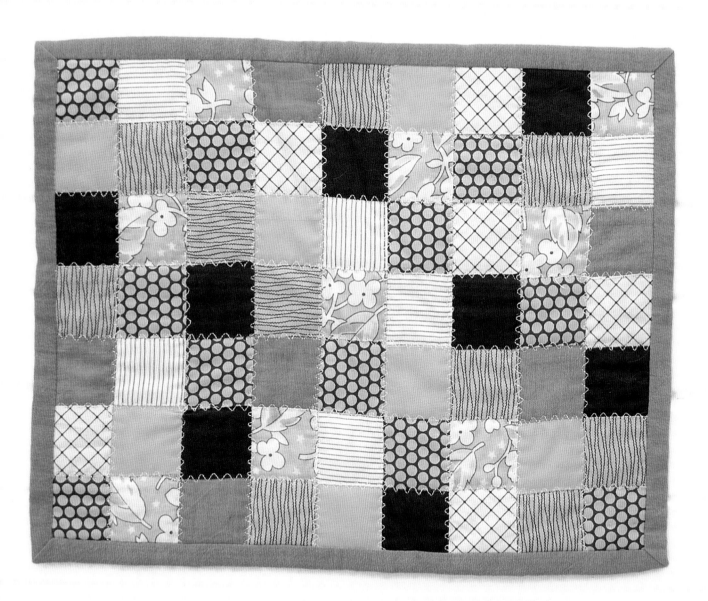

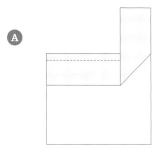

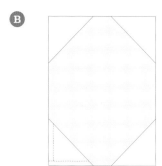

8. Set your sewing machine to sew a wavy line if you can (if you don't have a wavy stitch, use a zigzag or a straight stitch). Practice on a scrap of batting, adjusting the stitches to be about ⅛ inch wide and long so that the line looks like the perforated edge of a postage stamp.

   Quilt a wavy line using the stitch you've practiced over all the seams on your quilt top, removing the safety pins as you sew.

9. Trim the backing and batting even with the edges of the quilt top.

10. Beginning partway along one side of the quilt sandwich, lay the binding strip right side down, with one long edge matching the edge of the quilt top. Secure the strip with a couple of pins.

11. Leaving 2 inches of the binding free, start stitching ⅜ inch in from the edge.

12. As you approach the corner, stop and place a pin ⅜ inch from the bottom edge of the quilt top. Continue sewing until you reach the pin; then stop and backstitch (see page 130).

13. Take the quilt out of the machine, and turn it 90 degrees so that the sewn binding runs across the top edge. Fold the binding fabric up at a 45-degree angle to the corner (see Diagram A).

Then fold the fabric back down and line it up with the right edge of the quilt top; this will create a neat mitered corner.

14. Beginning at the edge of the quilt top, stitch ⅜ inch in from the right edge of the quilt top.

15. Repeat steps 12, 13, and 14 for the remaining three corners. Stop sewing about 3 inches away from the spot where you started sewing the binding down.

16. Fold both free ends of the binding back on themselves so that the fold lines meet. Press the fold lines lightly.

17. Fold the quilt top out of the way. Pin the two ends with right sides together and sew along the fold lines. Trim the seam allowances to ¼ inch, and press them open.

18. Reposition the binding in place, and finish sewing the binding to the quilt.

19. Add Fast-Finish Triangles to the back of the quilt to make hanging the quilt easy: Fold and press each of the four 3¾-inch squares in half diagonally with the wrong sides together. On the back of the quilt, place a folded triangle in each corner, aligning the raw edges of the quilt and triangle, and, from the quilt's right side, pin the triangles in place (see Diagram B).

20. On the right side of the quilt, sew over the stitches holding the binding in one corner to attach the first triangle (removing the pins as you come to them), but don't sew into the mitered fold—stop just before it, just as you did when attaching the binding. Next take the quilt out of the machine, cut the threads, and turn the quilt 90 degrees. Reinsert the quilt under the presser foot; and, beginning at the quilt's edge, sew along the second side of the triangle, taking care to follow the stitching line you made when stitching the binding's first edge.

21. Repeat step 20 with the other three triangles.

22. Turn the quilt over and fold the binding on itself so its raw edge meets the quilt's raw edges. Fold the folded binding over the edge of the quilt, hiding the stitching line, and pin it in place.

23. Slipstitch (see page 131) the binding in place by hand.

24. To hang the quilt, insert a wooden dowel (or chopstick) into the triangles at the top of the quilt and another into the lower two triangles. The top dowel will sit nicely on a nail, and the second one will keep the bottom edge of the quilt flat against the wall.

The Boise Peace Quilt Project

In the nineteenth century, American women, who could not vote, had to find other ways to express their political views. Often they turned to the traditional, communal, and sometimes subversive art of quilting to state their positions and to raise awareness and funding for political causes from abolition to prohibition. Famously, Susan B. Anthony made her first speech calling for women's suffrage at a quilting bee. In the late twentieth century, a group of women in Boise, Idaho became concerned by the Soviet-American arms race and the possibility of nuclear war. Faced with a threat too big to solve through ordinary political means, they resorted—like so many women before them—to quilting as a means of provocation, publicity, and persuasion.

In 1981, Anne Hausrath and Diane Jones attended a lecture given by Janet Gordon, an antinuclear activist. Gordon had grown up in Utah, downwind of the nuclear proving ground where nearly 200 atomic bombs were tested during the 1950s; her brother had died of cancer due to radiation exposure. "Here was this nice, patriotic woman whose whole life has been changed by nuclear weapons," Diane said in a 1986 interview. "I turned to Anne and said, 'Someone ought to do something,' and she said, 'Why don't we?'"

At the time, an all-out nuclear war with the Soviet Union seemed frighteningly possible. How could two stay-at-home mothers in Boise do anything to avert such devastation? Imagining that women in the Soviet Union must be as concerned about their children's future as they were, Anne and Diane decided to make a quilt and send it as a well-publicized gesture of friendship to the residents of a Soviet city about Boise's size. The fact that neither of them knew how to quilt did not faze them. In an early pamphlet, they wrote, "The idea for the Peace Quilt arose from two strands of thought: How can we make friends with some ordinary Russian people? And wouldn't it be fun to quilt together?"

When Anne wrote to the Soviet Embassy in Washington, D.C., to ask if the Soviet Union would be willing to receive a gift of peace from a small group of American citizens, she received no answer. It took the intervention of former Idaho Senator Frank Church, but eventually they secured the promise of the Soviet cultural attaché to deliver the quilt to the U.S.S.R.

Eighteen women and one man came to the first meeting of the Boise Peace Quilters at Anne's house. Most of them had never quilted before, so the two experienced quilters present agreed to hold a workshop. That first quilt, "Of Idaho and Peace," took thirty-six people three months to make. Its thirty-five blocks captured glimpses of family life in Idaho and of the state's natural beauty, peaceful images unlikely to be misinterpreted or censored. Heidi Reed, a young mother who had recently moved to Boise, had been "really despairing about the future and the chances for my kids' lives." She was thrilled when she heard about the peace quilt, but all of the squares had already been assigned to other quilters. At the last minute, when another quilter missed the deadline, Heidi stayed up all night to finish a replacement square. It was worth the missed sleep. "It just dried up all my despair," Heidi says. "It expanded my vision of what the future could be."

It took some diplomacy to keep the quilt out of a Leningrad museum, but the quilters persisted, and in the end it was displayed at the offices of the Soviet Women's Peace Committee in Moscow and then, just as they had hoped, in a smaller city in Lithuania.

The Boise Peace Quilters went on to create two or three quilts a year for more than a quarter century, all in the service of peace. They gave a friendship quilt to the people of Hiroshima, for example. "Our government had never made any [kind] of a statement that would indicate any… remorse for the destruction of the atomic bomb—certainly not an apology to the people of Japan," Diane Jones told an interviewer in 1986. "So we felt it was appropriate and important for ordinary Americans to make that statement." They collaborated with Soviet women on two quilts. And they made a National Peace Quilt, with one square from each of the fifty states, each bearing a child's hand-drawn interpretation of peace. They convinced eighty U.S. Senators to sleep for a night each beneath the quilt and to record their thoughts upon waking in a logbook. "We offer this quilt to our elected leaders," the quilters wrote in a letter that accompanied the quilt, "in the hope that the everyday act of sleeping beneath it will enable them to experience the power of our hopes and dreams for our children, the weight of our concerns for the future, and the serious challenge of their responsibility to our children."

66

Children must convince their elders to save the world, for without their guidance, their elders may lose it.

99

SENATOR JOHN WARNER
of Virginia, after spending a night sleeping beneath the National Peace Quilt in 1984

> **The patchwork quilt is really a symbol of the world which must come: one new design made out of many old designs. We will stitch this world together yet. Don't give up.**
>
> PETE SEEGER

Many of the Boise Peace Quilts were created to honor individuals for their peacemaking work. Longtime Peace Quilt volunteer Lyn McCollum says, "We don't have money to give people a million dollars, like the Nobel Peace Prize does. All we can do is make a work of art for them." And so they do. Each quilt is a magnificent piece of folk art and a carefully planned meditation on the peacemaker's work.

Any member of the Boise Peace Quilt Project can propose a recipient for a quilt. When the group meets to choose their next project, they listen to four or five proposals. Instead of voting on which project to pursue, the quilters sit in a circle and talk them over until they come to a consensus. Whoever proposes a quilt usually leads the design process. Many of the peacemaker quilts are built around a center medallion. Each surrounding block's design then relates to the work of the person being honored, and often the fabric and techniques do as well. William McDonough's quilt, for example, included bioengineered eco-friendly polyesters he and a chemist had developed to replenish the earth when they degrade. When the quilters made a quilt for Charlie Clements, a doctor who hiked through El Salvador to bring medical aid to local people during the wars in the 1980s, the quilters used reverse appliqué, a technique often employed by indigenous craftspeople in Central America.

Jinny DeFoggi, an artist and former teacher, joined the group during the making of the second quilt. "I would have been involved with the first one had I known about it," she says. "They were doing two of my favorite things to do in the world—they were working for peace, and they were making art." Pete Seeger's quilt was Jinny's idea; he's one of her "since-the-sixties heroes." She made the center medallion for the quilt and went to San Francisco with another quilter to present it to him at a concert.

Each quilt requires about 10,000 hours of planning and hands-on work. To the quilters, the collaborative creative process and the fun they have working together have always been as important as the final quilt. "It was also a little subversive, which I liked," Heidi says; the fact that needle-work wasn't an expected political tool gave it extra power.

Several hundred quilters have contributed to the quilts over the years, but a small core of dedicated peacemakers have stayed with the project since its early days. They're a close-knit group, and they've seen each other through many personal as well as political ups and downs. As they enter a new phase in their lives—several are grandmothers now—they're considering the future of their project. "We don't have the same kind of energy that created three quilts in a year," Heidi says. "We're slowing down, but no one is willing to let go of the human connections. No one is willing to let go of the hope."

Hope has always been at the center of the Boise Peace Quilt Project's work. "We've always tried to use the way we make quilts to change the place where we live, to challenge people's idea of how life works," Heidi says. "We've tried to set an example of cooperative creativity. We're really ordinary, and we've used simple tools, but we've had the determination to challenge power holders and the status quo. And if we could do that, it has huge implications for other ordinary people." Heidi's children, Tobias and Hannah, were little when the first quilt was made. Nearly three decades later, despite an environmental crisis as great as the nuclear threat that once provoked their mother to action, "they have emerged as grown-ups who are not depressed about the future...who never faltered from thinking they could change things." That alone, Heidi says, is worth every moment she has ever spent quilting. ✳

BOISE PEACE QUILT RECIPIENTS

The following individuals have all received Boise Peace Quilts to honor their peacemaking work:

ROSA PARKS
civil rights pioneer (and quilter)

NORMAN COUSINS
journalist and peace activist

PETE SEEGER
folk singer

JOHN JEVONS
ecologist

EVE ENSLER
playwright

WILLIAM MCDONOUGH
architect

DR. HELEN CALDICOTT
antinuclear activist

CÉSAR CHÁVEZ
labor organizer

FRANK CHURCH
United States senator

JULIA BUTTERFLY
environmental activist

Blanket the Globe

Casey Ehrlich, a high school junior in Marblehead, Massachusetts, remembers watching the evening news with her mother and her eleven-year-old sister, Jamie, on Earth Day 2007. The news about the environment was depressing. "At first I felt kind of hopeless," she says, "and I thought that I might not be the only one that felt that way. Maybe other kids felt hopeless and even worse, powerless. I wanted to do something about that, because the first step to making change is to influence others to join in." Casey has always loved making art, so the first idea that popped into her head was an art project that would let kids express their anxiety about the environment. At first she imagined a montage of children's drawings, but she wanted something more permanent that didn't use all that paper. So she turned to quilting.

After gathering recycled fabric and fleece and convincing her friends and sister to join in, Casey realized something: she didn't know how to sew. Neither did her mother. So they bought a sewing machine and taught themselves how to use it. "You can see our gradual improvement through the quilts," Casey says.

Casey's mother, Lori, a Massachusetts State Representative, is one of three people who inspired her to start her quilt project (the others are biologist and activist Jane Goodall and former Vice-President Al Gore). "I've always grown up in an environmentally cautious house," Casey explains. "From when I was around four years old, my mom's been really environmentally active. She got started on environmental issues when I came running in from our deck and my little feet were covered in black soot. It ended up being from the power plant, and that really got her started about 'How do we power-wash our lungs?'"

Casey let her sister Jamie make the first square: "She had this fleece pair of polar bear pajama pants, and they got a little too small on her, so we cut one of the polar bears out and we put it on a piece of blue fabric." Casey made the second square herself. Neither sister has made another square since. "You're only allowed to make one," Casey says. "The square represents a kid's voice, and I wouldn't want one kid to have more say than another."

After she created a website for her project and advertised it elsewhere on the web, Casey began receiving e-mails and quilt squares from all over the world. Locally, she visited classrooms and Brownie, Girl Scout, and Boy Scout troops to spread the word about her idea.

To make squares for the quilt, kids start with twelve-inch squares of recycled fabric. Casey asks them to use fabric paints, markers, and embellishments to make designs that show how they feel connected to the environment and how they think they can help it. Many of Casey's favorites of the squares she's collected so far include animals. One depicts a rectangular-shaped pig with a square head; underneath the artist wrote, "Be nice to pigs." Another one, with a picture of a little dog, urges, "Save the Chihuahuas." Surprisingly, all the kids she encounters—even four- and five-year-olds—already know about global warming. "It's great to have kids educated about it at that age," Casey says, "but if you don't present them with a solution or the idea of a possible solution, then that does create some anxiety. I'd really like to help kids and let them know that there's a way to solve this, and that we can change."

In the first year and a half, Casey gathered more than 2,000 squares. She and a handful of volunteers sewed them into panels of about fifty, which she displays, a few at a time (all that will fit in the family car) wherever she can: at parks, festivals, farmers' markets, and even backstage at the 2007 Live Earth USA benefit concert at Giants Stadium in New Jersey. In 2008, the quilt appeared at the Massachusetts State House in Boston; one day she wants to take it to the National Mall in Washington, D.C. Often, people who see the quilt ask if their own kids can participate. Sometimes Casey will set a date to return to the same spot with materials for a square-making gathering.

Like many quilters, Casey thinks of her project in terms of its small, yet real effect on each individual it touches. She says, "My ideal goal would be if, before someone went to throw a piece of garbage on the ground, they really thought about it. Like, 'Where is this going, can I prevent this, what can I do?' If they didn't throw that piece of garbage and they put it in the trash or the recycling, then I think my project is a success." That may sound like a modest goal. But multiply that awareness and sense of responsibility by the 2,000-plus kids who've participated so far, and all those who will in the future, and the many adults who will be moved by the quilt, and you get the beginning of the kind of change the planet needs. ✺

HOW YOU CAN HELP

Encourage a child you know to make a square. Casey recommends practicing on paper first, before creating final designs on 12-inch squares of nonstretchy, durable cotton fabric (recycled if possible). Many techniques will work, such as patchwork, fabric pens or permanent markers (Sharpies can bleed on some fabrics—be sure to test them first), fabric paints (Casey recommends Tulip matte paints), appliqué, collage, and iron-on photo transfers.

If you live in or near Massachusetts, volunteer to assemble panels.

Donate supplies such as fabric, fake fur, decals, computer supplies for transfers, and fabric pens (or donate money for supplies).

Contact Casey at **casey@blankettheglobe.net** to arrange shipping completed squares and donated supplies.

For more information, visit Casey's website, **www.blankettheglobe.net**.

CHAPTER FIVE

Getting Involved

There's no reason not to start quilting for peace right now. You don't need to have any quilting experience, and you don't need to make a huge commitment. If you make just one quilt a year—or one quilt ever—and donate it, you can bring comfort and warmth to someone who needs it badly or make someone stop and think about an issue about which you care deeply. Many of the groups in this book even accept single quilt blocks or raw quilt tops.

You can quilt for peace by yourself and donate to a local organization, or to someone you know or hear about who has fallen ill or on hard times. But if you're looking for camaraderie, support, and perhaps a little help with your sewing skills, there's nothing better than joining a group of quilters working together for a good cause.

HOW TO FIND A QUILTING-FOR-PEACE GROUP

Reading about the organizations and individuals profiled in this book is a great way to start quilting for peace. To expand your research, a web search engine, like Google, is the best next step. These days, nearly every quilting group has its own website. To locate a group, try searching with the words *charity, war,* and *peace,* along with *quilt* or *quilting.* Be sure to search blogs as well as websites. Also search Yahoo, Google, and Facebook groups—quilters have formed active communities on all three sites.

Quilting guilds almost always participate in community service quilting efforts. Guild members may also be able to put you in touch with local groups that quilt for peace as well as organizations that need donated quilts. To find a quilting guild near you, visit www.quiltguilds.com. Fabric shops are another good source of information about quilting groups in your community. Ask for recommendations and check the bulletin board, if there is one.

HOW TO START YOUR OWN QUILTING-FOR-PEACE GROUP

Make a Plan
Have a serious think about what you want to accomplish. Who needs your help most? What social or political issue feels most urgent to you? The more passionate you are about your work, the more persuasive you will be and the more you will get done.

Find out if other quilters are working on the same issues. If so, consider joining or collaborating with an existing group. If you decide to start your own group, make sure its purpose is simple and specific enough to explain in a sentence or two. That will help you stay focused and convince others to help or donate.

Consider how quilts can help solve the problem—both practically and symbolically. Design your project so that it's accessible to beginning quilters yet interesting to those who are more experienced. And keep the requirements flexible to give quilters a chance to be creative.

You'll need to find volunteers as well as partners who can help you distribute the quilts, and the Internet has made this job easy and nearly free. Set up a website, start an online group, or launch a blog. Visit and comment on other craft blogs to encourage others to come to yours. As your group grows, send regular e-mail updates to your volunteers and encourage them to forward the e-mails to others.

Write a short article about your organization and send it to your local newspaper. Be sure to include photos—pictures of people receiving quilts are the most powerful. Small newspapers are often especially happy to run stories about local groups doing interesting things.

Use old-fashioned word of mouth. Let local fabric stores and quilting guilds know about your group's activities. Post flyers wherever crafters may gather. Tell everyone who will listen about what you're doing. In your network of friends-of-friends, there are probably quite a few crafters.

Find Donations

Most quilters buy more fabric than they can possibly use, so it isn't usually hard to convince them to part with a few yards for a good cause. Put up a sign in your local quilt store asking for fabric donations. Many quilting-for-peace groups receive fabric donations from families of quilters who have died and left a legacy of fabric behind. While it could be awkward to seek out that sort of donation, by making as many quilters aware of your need as possible, you'll increase the odds of people who want to donate fabric finding you.

The textile, clothing, and interior design industries discard a huge amount of fabric. Contact fabric companies, clothing manufacturers, and design showrooms and ask for donations of samples, offcuts, or discontinued material. Quilting fabric or supply companies may be willing to donate materials in return for publicity, as well.

Try contacting nearby hotels or resorts to find out if they'd be willing to donate clean, used sheets to be used as quilt backings (hotels are required by law to replace bedding regularly). In some cities, a government agency or nonprofit group, such as Freecycle (www.freecycle.org), collects donated art materials (including fabric) from businesses and makes them available to public schools and community organizations.

Choose How Much to Grow

As your group grows, you will need to decide how large and formal you want to become. In order to accept monetary donations and seek grants, you'll need to apply for nonprofit status. But becoming a nonprofit organization presents some challenges: The application process can be costly, and nonprofits are required to do a lot of paperwork—you'll need to keep detailed records, provide annual reports, and file documents with state agencies on a regular basis. The Foundation Center (www.foundationcenter.org) is a good source of information on the pros and cons of applying for nonprofit status.

There are other considerations as well. How much time do you want to spend on administration versus other activities? Do you want to coordinate multiple chapters and thousands of volunteers? How much control are you comfortable giving up? Some founders like to keep a close eye on their organizations' efforts, while others are thrilled when quilters start putting their ideas into practice in other places. Decide how far-reaching you want to be, and if you would mind others adapting your ideas to local needs. You may even decide that you don't want to grow at all, and that you would prefer your group to stay small and local.

BASIC QUILTING TOOL KIT

Below you'll find the basic tool kit needed for the projects in this book. Additional supplies required will be noted in a supplies list at the beginning of the project.

Chalk fabric marker

My favorite marking tool is the Clover Chaco Liner, available at www.clover-usa.com. It makes accurate lines that are easy to remove. I find that silver chalk pens show on most fabrics.

Curved hand-sewing needle with large eye

Several of the projects in this book call for tying the quilt sandwich together with square knots (see page 132). A curved hand-sewing needle with a large eye makes tying a quilt much easier.

Quilter's ruler

Quilter's rulers are transparent or translucent and marked at 1/8-inch intervals to make it easy to cut fabric accurately without needing to line it up perfectly on your cutting mat. These rulers are also marked with diagonal lines at 30, 45, and 60 degrees to help you cut triangles and diamonds. I find it useful to have both a long, narrow quilter's ruler (22 inches x 6 inches) and a square quilter's ruler. If you buy only one quilter's ruler, choose a 12 1/2-inch square one.

Quilter's safety pins

Curved quilter's safety pins make pinning a quilt sandwich (see page 128) much easier. These safety pins are sold in several sizes; I use size 1.

Rotary cutter and cutting mat

A rotary cutter makes cutting fabric pieces fast, accurate, and easy. You can buy rotary cutters with different size blades; I find that the 45mm size works for everything I need to do. Replace the blade often; you should be able to cut through several layers of fabric in a single stroke. And while cutting, remember always to move the blade away from your body. When using a rotary cutter, protect your table with a cutting mat. Quilter's cutting mats are marked with grids and diagonal lines to help you align and cut pieces accurately. Your mat should be at least 18 inches x 24 inches.

Seam ripper

If you've made a mistake and need to rip out your seams, a seam ripper is an enormously helpful tool. Be sure that your seam ripper is sharp. When it's dull, replace it.

Sewing machine

You'll obviously need a sewing machine, but you don't need a fabulous, expensive "sewing computer"—a simple, used machine will do fine. A walking foot is a helpful addition to your machine for machine-quilting—it keeps a quilt's three layers from shifting as you sew—and a darning foot is also useful for meander-quilting (see page 130).

Sewing scissors

You'll need sewing scissors for cutting fabric. Never use them for cutting paper, which will cause them to grow dull fast.

FINISHING A QUILT

After piecing a quilt top, you'll need to finish the quilt. This involves layering and pinning the quilt top, batting, and backing to make a quilt sandwich; machine-quilting the layers or hand-tying them together to keep them from shifting; and binding the quilt.

1. Make a quilt sandwich

To prepare for layering the quilt top, batting, and backing into a quilt sandwich, first press the finished quilt top. Piece the backing, if necessary, and press the seams to one side. Since the quilting process itself can cause the backing and batting to shrink a little, make sure to cut the backing and batting about 4 inches larger all around than the quilt top itself. You'll trim away any excess batting and backing fabric before binding the quilt.

To make the quilt sandwich, lay the backing on the floor or a big table, right side down, and smooth it out as much as possible. Using plenty of small pieces of masking or painter's tape, affix the fabric's edges to the floor (or table), adjusting both the fabric and the tape as you go, until the entire backing is smooth. Next lay the batting on top of the backing, aligning the edges of both layers, and smooth the batting out. Finally lay the quilt top, right side up and centered, on top of the batting, and smooth it out.

2. Pin the quilt sandwich

Traditionally the layers of a quilt sandwich are basted or temporarily secured with a needle and thread to prepare them for permanently quilting or tying them together (Step 3), but it's much easier to baste the layers by pinning them with quilters' safety pins (see page 127). Because these safety pins are curved, they are easier to use than regular safety pins. To pin-baste, begin pinning at the center of the quilt and work outward, smoothing the quilt as you go and placing the pins no more than 5 inches apart.

3. Machine-quilt or hand-tie the layers together

There are two options used in this book for permanently securing the layers of a quilt sandwich: stitching by machine or hand-tying. When planning a quilting pattern for a patchwork quilt top, decide whether you want to play up or counterbalance the patchwork pattern. To emphasize the patchwork's piecing, consider outline-quilting (stitching about ¼ inch away from the seams between pieces). To unify the pattern, choose an allover grid pattern (with quilting lines no more than 5 inches apart) or a meandering pattern (see Meander-quilting on page 130). However you choose to machine-quilt, be sure that the density of quilting is roughly the same across the whole quilt.

If you want to hand-tie the quilt sandwich (making it technically a comforter, not a quilt), use a curved hand-sewing needle with a large eye and pearl cotton (I like pearl cotton rather than embroidery floss since it's a little thicker and the strands don't separate quite as easily). To make each tie, insert your needle from the front to the back of the quilt sandwich, and then bring the needle up again on the front of the sandwich as close as possible to the point where you originally inserted it. Make a square knot (see page 132), pulling the threads firmly; and then trim the thread tails about ½ inch away from the knot. Position the ties in a grid, no more than 5 inches apart.

4. Bind the quilt

There are two ways to bind a quilt: with a traditional binding, using a separate strip of binding fabric, and with a mock binding, folding the backing fabric over the edge of the quilt top. Mock bindings are much faster, but traditional bindings are more durable and allow you to use contrasting binding and backing fabrics.

To make a traditional binding

Begin by trimming the batting and backing even with the quilt top. Next cut 2¼-inch-deep, bias-cut strips (strips cut diagonally across the fabric's grain). To determine the total length of bias strips you'll need to bind your quilt, measure the quilt top's perimeter and add 10 inches. Cut the binding fabric into diagonal strips, and piece them together, as described below, to create a very long strip.

Sew the strips together end to end, using a ¼-inch diagonal seam (so the strips lie flatter). To join two strips, pin them right sides together and perpendicular to each other, letting the ends overlap a little (see Diagram A). Mark a diagonal line beginning and ending at the points where the two strips intersect. Sew along this line; then trim the ends of the strips, leaving a ¼-inch seam allowance. Press the seam allowances open to reduce bulk (see Seam allowances, pressing on page 132). Fold the completed binding strip in half lengthwise, with wrong sides together and the raw edges aligned, and press the fold.

To attach the folded binding to the quilt sandwich, start positioning it about at the midpoint of one side of the quilt, aligning the raw edges of the binding and quilt. Leave about 3 inches of the binding free, and then pin a few inches of binding to the quilt. Check to be sure that none of the seams in your binding will fall at corners of the quilt. If it seems likely that a binding seam will fall at the corner, unpin the binding, move it a few inches along the quilt edge, and re-pin it in place.

Attach your walking foot, if you have one, to your machine, and sew the binding to the quilt with a ¼-inch seam. When you arrive ¼ inch from the corner, stop, with the needle down in your fabric, and backstitch (see page 130) to secure your stitching. Remove the quilt from the machine, and cut the threads.

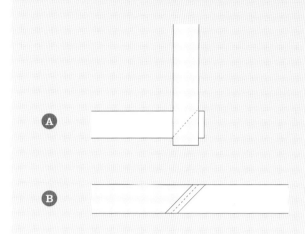

To make a neat corner, fold the strip straight up, so that its right edge is aligned with the edge of the quilt and its bottom end forms a 45-degree angle (see Diagram A on page 116). Then fold the strip back down so that the fold matches the top of the quilt exactly. Reposition the quilt in the machine, and lower the presser foot and needle. Then, beginning at the edge of the quilt, continue sewing the binding, taking care to maintain a ¼-inch seam. As you reach each corner, repeat the steps above.

Stop sewing about 4 inches away from where you started attaching the binding, and backstitch a couple of stitches. Leave about 5 inches of binding free, and trim away the rest of the binding strip. Unfold the beginning of the binding, and cut it at a 45-degree angle. Unfold the end of the binding, lay the binding's beginning end over this unfolded end, and trim the bottom binding strip parallel to the top strip, leaving the bottom strip ¼ inch longer than the top one. Place the ends right sides together, and sew with a ¼-inch seam. Refold the binding wrong sides together, pin it to the quilt, and finish attaching it. Fold the binding to the back of the quilt, taking care to turn all four corners neatly, and pin the binding in place. Sew the binding down by hand, using a slipstitch (see page 131).

To make a mock binding

Machine-baste around the whole quilt sandwich ⅛ inch in from the edge of the quilt top, using the longest stitch your machine will allow. Trim the batting to ¼ inch larger all around than the edge of the quilt top, taking care not to snip the backing fabric as you cut the batting. Trim the backing fabric 1 inch larger all around than the batting.

Fold each corner of the backing fabric over each corner of the batting and quilt top at a 45-degree angle to the corner, so that the center of the fold just meets the corner of the quilt top, and press the fold. Beginning at one corner, fold the edge of the backing on itself so that its raw edge meets the edge of the quilt top, and press the fold. Then wrap this folded edge over the batting and quilt top and pin it in place. Continue working around the quilt, pinning the binding down and ensuring that the diagonally folded ends meet at neat 45-degree angles at each corner (these are mitered corners). Cut out the small square of extra backing fabric that shows beneath the binding at each corner.

Edge-stitch (see right) the binding as close to the folded edge as you can (an edge-stitching foot for your sewing machine is a huge help here), lockstitching or backstitching (see right) at the beginning and end of your stitching.

Remove the basting stitches near the edge of the quilt top on the back of the quilt. Slipstitch the corners closed by hand.

STITCHES

Backstitch Backstitching by machine is a way to secure the stitches at the beginning and end of a seam line. To backstitch at the start of a seam, position the needle in the fabric a couple stitches ahead of where the seam is to begin, press your machine's reverse button, and sew several stitches in reverse back to the seam's starting point. Release the reverse button, stitch forward over the backstitches, and continue sewing the seam. To backstitch at the end of a seam, press the reverse button, and sew several stitches in reverse over the seam's last stitches.

Edge-stitch As its name implies, edge-stitching involves stitching very close—about 1/16 inch to ⅛ inch—to the fabric's folded or cut edge (compare with Topstitch at right).

Lockstitch This is an easy and essentially invisible way to secure a seam. To lockstitch at the beginning of a seam, set the stitch length near zero and take a couple of stitches in place; then reset the stitch length to its regular setting and sew as you normally would. When you reach the end of the seam, again set the stitch length near zero and take a couple stitches in place before removing the fabric from under the needle.

Meander-quilt This freestyle machine-quilting technique is used for filling in an area of a quilt or for quilting an allover pattern. To meander-quilt, first lower your feed dogs, and use a darning foot on your machine if you have one. Then stitch continuous, wandering, wavy lines about 1 inch to 2 inches apart that never cross each other, lockstitching (see above) at the beginning and end of each seam to secure the stitches. Sew at a medium to fast pace, but move your hands slowly and smoothly to keep the stitches even. Learning to meander-quilt takes a little practice, but once you get used to it, it isn't hard.

Outline-quilt Stitch ¼ inch inside the seam lines of the pieces of your pattern that you want to accentuate, lockstitching (see left) at the beginning and end of each seam to secure the stitches.

Slipstitch This stitch creates an almost invisible seam between two folded edges or between a folded edge and the flat fabric to which it's sewn. Use a slipstitch to finish bindings and to close hems after turning comforters right side out or stuffing toys.

To sew a slipstitch, start by bringing the needle up from the fabric's wrong side through one folded edge, and pull the thread through. Insert the needle into the second folded edge or the flat fabric just opposite the stitch in the first fold, taking a very small bite of the fabric, and pull the thread through. Repeat this stitch on the first fold, and continue taking a tiny stitch on one side and then the other until you finish the seam.

Stitch-in-the-ditch Stitching-in-the-ditch refers to stitching directly over a seam line or very close—¹⁄₁₆ inch to ⅛ inch—to it. In quilting, stitching-in-the-ditch is often used over the seam lines in patchwork to emphasize the pieced pattern. Using a walking foot on your machine will help keep the layers of the quilt sandwich flat and your stitching even as you stitch-in-the-ditch. Be sure to lockstitch (see left) at the beginning and end of each seam to secure your stitches.

Topstitch This stitch involves stitching more than ⅛ inch—from ¼ inch to several inches—away from the fabric's cut or folded edge. Topstitching is used to reinforce an edge, attach an appliqué, or decorate a surface (compare with Edge-stitch at left).

Bias tape This tape is a narrow strip of fabric cut on the diagonal that's folded and pressed either once (single-fold) or twice (double-fold). Since the fabric is cut diagonally, it is more flexible and durable than if it were cut on the straight grain. Bias tape is often used for binding baby blankets and bibs. When I buy bias tape, I always choose double-fold tape to avoid having to fold and iron it again myself. If you can't find readymade tape you like, you can buy a bias tape maker and, with only a little extra work (following the directions that come with the tape maker), make it yourself.

Chain-piecing This technique is a shortcut to use when joining many identical pieces of fabric into pairs. To chain-piece a series of pairs, after sewing the first two pieces together, stop sewing, but don't lift up the needle. Push the next pair of pieces up to the presser foot, and continue sewing. Keep repeating these steps until you've chain-pieced all the pairs. Then snip the threads between each pair before pressing the seam allowances.

Fat quarter A fat quarter of fabric gets its name from the way that it's cut from the bolt. Instead of dividing a yard of 44-inch-wide fabric into four narrow ("nonfat") quarter-yard strips, a quarter yard is made by cutting the yard in half twice, first lengthwise (making two 18-inch x 44-inch cuts) and then across the width (making four 18-inch x 22-inch pieces, or fat quarters).

Interfacing Available in many varieties and weights, interfacing is an extra layer of fabric that adds stability and structure to another fabric. Iron-on fusible interfacing is good for appliqué and for counteracting the stretchiness of some fabrics so that they can be used in patchwork projects. I like Steam-a-Seam2 because it's a little sticky on both sides.

Pin-basting See Step 2 of "Finishing a quilt" on page 128.

Seam allowance A seam's allowance is the distance between the seam line's stitches and the fabric's raw or folded edge. Patchwork calls for a ¼-inch seam (that is, a seam that's sewn ¼ inch from the fabric's edge and hence has ¼-inch seam allowances), unless a pattern states otherwise. If a ¼-inch guideline isn't marked clearly on the bed of your sewing machine, mark it yourself with a little piece of masking tape.

Seam allowances, pressing Generally speaking, in sewing, a seam's allowances can be pressed open in opposite directions or pressed together as a unit to one side of the seam line. In quilting, seam allowances are usually pressed together to one side, rather than open, to prevent fuzzy bits of batting from sneaking through the seam line after lots of laundering. Usually seam allowances should be pressed to the side of the darker fabric, which helps prevent them from being seen. The project directions will always indicate whether the allowances are to be pressed open or to one side.

Selvedge Woven fabric comes off the loom on which it's manufactured with extra-tightly woven edges about ½ inch wide along the sides of the yardage. These edges are called selvedges. Because selvedges aren't usable in quilting, you'll need to trim them away before cutting your fabric into the pieces required for the project.

Snipping corners A worthwhile extra step to take before prewashing fabric, snipping off a little triangle from each corner of a piece of fabric prevents the threads from unraveling and knotting in the washer and dryer.

Square knot To tie a square knot (also called a double knot), tie the two thread tails just as you would for the first step of tying a shoelace; then repeat the process a second time.

Squaring up When piecing quilt blocks, it's easy to end up with blocks that aren't perfectly square. It's a good idea to trim the sides of each block a tiny bit so that they're even and at right angles to each other. This extra step, called squaring up, makes it easier to sew the blocks together accurately. Squaring up is especially important when you're dealing with triangles, as in the Preemie Pinwheel Quilt on page 70. Several of the patterns in this book call for making blocks slightly larger than needed and then trimming them to the right size.

Squaring up the blocks as you make them usually means that your quilt top will end up even enough, and you won't need to square up the whole thing. Don't worry if your quilt top isn't a perfect rectangle. A little crookedness adds character. If the quilt top's edges are really uneven, however, slip a cutting mat under one corner and use your square quilter's ruler (see page 127) to even it up. Then slide the cutting mat along one side of the quilt, using your 24-inch x 6-inch quilter's ruler to trim it slightly (but don't be tempted to over-trim, especially if the pieced pattern extends to the edges of the quilt top). Switch to the square quilter's ruler at each corner, and continue trimming until you have squared up the whole quilt top.

Strip-piecing This is a quick method of cutting and piecing squares (or rectangles or diamonds). Instead of cutting out individual pieces of fabric and then sewing them together into blocks, sew selvedge-to-selvedge strips together first, and then cut them into ready-pieced partial blocks.

RECOMMENDED READING

The Purl Bee
www.purlbee.com
The Purl Bee is an online craft journal written by the owners and employees of Purl Patchwork and its sister yarn shop, Purl, in New York City. They've posted loads of useful tutorials and project instructions.

True Up
www.trueup.net
A great blog all about fabric written by longtime craft blogger Kim Kight. Good for inspiration, as well as finding out about sales and new designs.

Whip Up
www.whipup.net
Reading Whipup is a good way to keep track of what the online crafting community is up to.

HISTORICAL READING
I consulted the following excellent sources while researching the history of quilting-for-peace efforts.

Crib Quilts and Other Small Wonders
Thomas K. Woodward and Blanche Greenstein
E.P. Dutton

Hearts and Hands: The Influence of Women and Quilts on American Society
Pat Ferrero, Elaine Hedges, and Julie Silber
The Quilt Digest Press

Patchwork: Iowa Quilts and Quilters
Jacqueline Andre Schmeal
University of Iowa Press

"Quilts for Union Soldiers in the Civil War" in Uncoverings, volume 6 of the research papers of the American Quilt Study Group
Virginia Gunn

Quilts from the Civil War
Barbara Brackman
C&T Publishing

Tactical Textiles: A Genealogy of the Boise Peace Quilt Project: 1981–1988
Angeline Kearns Blain
Kendall/Hunt Publishing Company

SOURCES FOR SUPPLIES
Purl Patchwork supplied almost all of the fabric and batting used in this book. It's where I do as much of my fabric shopping as I possibly can, even though I don't live in New York. It is a tiny store filled with one of the best fabric collections I have ever encountered, and the website, www.purlsoho.com, is the next best thing to visiting the store in person.

Purl Patchwork
147 Sullivan Street
New York, NY 10012
(212) 420-8798
www.purlsoho.com

I used cotton batting from Quilter's Dream for all the projects in this book. Following is a list of most of the fabrics I used. Fabric lines change frequently, and fabrics imported from Japan are especially difficult for shops to keep in stock, so some of the exact prints listed below may not be readily available. However, if you are looking for a particular fabric found in this book, this will help you identify the producer and perhaps find a similar fabric.

Four-Patch Comfort, page 10
Moda, Cake Rock Beach, Earth Fisherman 25018-33 and Earth Sand 25014-31; Rowan Fabrics, Kaffe Fassett Shot Cotton, Brick 58; Windham Fabrics, Farmhouse Blues, 24262, 24249, and 28179-5

Recycled Sleeping Bag, page 19
Kokka Fabrics, Black Trees HA3420-24D

Pink Ribbon String Quilt, page 24
Yuwa Fabrics, Sheer Dots, Grey PD814F; Windham Fabrics, Miniatures, 25854-1 and 25854-14; Windham Fabrics, Williamsburg Centennial Collection, 27205-1; Olympus, Soleil, Pink Rose; Kokka Fabrics, Nani Iro, Iro Muji, and Dove Grey

Cage Comforters, page 30
Seven Islands, Puppy Command, Natural 2000-1A; Robert Kaufman, Essex, Pompeii Red, Orange, and Red

Civil War Album Quilt, page 38
Windham Fabrics, New Nation, Turquoise Dancing Roots 26826-2; Windham Fabrics, Civil War V, Blue Floral Scroll 27333-1 and Blue Wheat 27334-1; Windham Fabrics, Old Glory III, Navy Sundial Flower 27126-5

Sawtooth Star Quilt, page 48
Rowan Fabrics, Kaffe Fassett Shot Cotton, Sludge 57, Denim Blue 15, Smoky 20, Aegean 46, and Sky 62

Easy, Striped Baby Quilt, page 64
Kokka Fabrics, Country Landscape, Red HA3420-23B; Yuwa Fabrics, Honeycomb, Rust 111

Preemie Pinwheel Quilt, page 70
Olympus, Soleil, Red Kobai 4217; Yuwa Fabrics, Sheer Dots, Pink PD814A; Joel Dewberry, Aviary, Woodgrain, Orange JD-20; Windham Fabrics, Hannah Collection, Blue Stripe 28295-2

Bib and Matching Burp Cloth, page 76
Michael Miller, Organic Terry, Natural OC3618-NATU-D

Mirabel the Owl, page 85
Mary Flanagan wool felt, Luna Gold, Chestnut, and Old Crow; Rowan Fabrics, Kaffe Fassett Shot Cotton, Ginger 01; Yuwa, Patchwork Fruit, Green Squares HA3430-33C

Emergency Snuggle Quilt, page 90
Moda, Za Za, Butternut

Speedy Housetop Quilt, page 98
Yuwa Fabrics, Honeycomb, Yellow 102; Kokka Fabrics, Nani Iro, Pink Blooms JG8300-1C; Moda, Net of Jewels, Tourmaline 12551-20; Rowan Fabrics, Kaffe Fassett Shot Cotton, Blush 28

30-Minute Shopping Bag, page 106
Echino, Red Plane Squares JG99000-900C; Joel Dewberry, Ginseng, Celery Pine HDJD06, Glacier Bloom HDJD02, and Rust Wildflowers HDJD05; Seven Islands, Lotus Garden, Brown Damask PA20210-10C

Priority Alzheimer's Quilt, page 114
Yuwa Fabrics, Falling Leaves, Tan PD802-D; Moda, Cake Rock Beach, Water Honeycomb 25015-35 and Water Waves 25013-30

Acknowledgments

I am deeply grateful to the following people:

First and foremost, the quilters and organizers who appear in this book, whose hard work and dedication warm and comfort thousands of people. Without their generosity—and their willingness to share their time, stories, and patterns with me—this book could not exist. Also Cindy Windecker, Ann Philpot, Kristin Eno, June Nielsen, Elizabeth Shefrin, and Ina May Gaskin, all of whose work is just as inspiring.

At Stewart, Tabori & Chang, my editor Liana Allday, who expertly guided me through the process of putting this book together; Melanie Falick, who helped conceive and shape this project; Betty Christiansen, whose book *Knitting for Peace* was the model for this one and whose eye for detail clarified every chapter of mine; and Chris Timmons, without whom my patterns would make much less sense.

My agent, Andy McNicol, whose faith and enthusiasm never seem to waver.

Thayer Gowdy, whose photographs are lovely.

Joelle Hoverson, whose advice on choosing fabrics was invaluable and who generously supplied almost all the material I used in the book. Eva Jensen at Purl Patchwork and Rickie Painter at PurlSoho.com were also very helpful.

Ellen Sime, who put weeks of time and effort into quilting many of the projects in this book. I couldn't have finished the projects in time without Ellen's help.

Nancy Howard, who gave me exactly the advice I needed and pieced the Blue Star quilt beautifully and just in time.

Martha Supnik, librarian at the New England Quilt Museum, who helped with my early research.

Eric Hellweg, whose understanding and support made my writing and sewing schedule possible.

Megan Wycoff and Kate Mason, who gave me much-needed last-minute help.

My friends Michelle Falkoff, Amy Gallo, Don Lee, and Lisa Franzetta, who for years have given me the courage to write.

Moira Belle Callaghan Sansone, who inspired my very first quilt.

Nancy Mendoza, who taught me about design and gave me love and support throughout the making of this book.

And most of all, my parents, whose love, advice, humor, and faith have made everything, including this book, possible.

*Katherine Bell graduated from the Iowa Writers' Workshop,
and her fiction has been published in* Best American Short Stories.
*In her day job as an online editor, everything she does is digital;
to put herself back in the physical world she cooks and quilts.
She lives in Somerville, Massachusetts.*

Published in 2009 by Stewart, Tabori & Chang
An imprint of ABRAMS

Text copyright © 2009 by Katherine Bell
Photographs copyright © 2009 Thayer Allyson Gowdy

Library of Congress Cataloging-in-Publication Data:
Bell, Katherine, 1974
Quilting For Peace / by Katherine Bell; Photography by
Thayer Allyson Gowdy
        p. cm.
Includes bibliographical references and index.
ISBN 978-1-58479-804-0 (alk. paper)
  1. Patchwork. 2. Quiltmakers--United States. 3. Patchwork
quilts--United
States. I. Title.
  TT835.B3335 2009
  746.46--DC2

Editors: Liana Allday and Melanie Falick
Designer: Onethread Design
Technical Editor: Chris Timmons

The text of this book was composed in Neutraface Text, and Clarendon BT.

Printed and bound in China.
10 9 8 7 6 5 4 3 2 1

"'Hope' is the thing with feathers" reprinted by permission of the publishers
and Trustees of Amherst College from *The Poems of Emily Dickinson:
Variorum Edition*, Ralph W. Franklin, ed, Cambridge, Mass.: The Belknap
Press of Harvard University Press, Copyright © 1998 by the President and
Fellows of Harvard College. Copyright © 1951, 1955, 1979, 1983 by the
President and Fellows of Harvard College.

115 West 18th Street
New York, NY 10011
www.abramsbooks.com